TORAH PORTIONS FOR CHILDREN
B'reisheet
BOOK 1: GENESIS

NATALEE HENRY & YEVGENIYA CALENDRILLO

TORAH PORTIONS FOR CHILDREN
B'reisheet
BOOK 1: GENESIS

Natalee Henry & Yevgeniya Calendrillo

Copyright © Natalee Henry & Yevgeniya Calendrillo, 2023.

Printed in the United States 2023

All rights reserved. This book may not be copied or reprinted for commercial gain or profit. No portion of this book may be reproduced, stored in a retrieval system, transmitted in any form or by any means electronic, mechanical photocopy, recording, or any other except brief quotations in printed reviews, without the prior permission of the Authors and the Publisher. Rights for publishing this book in other languages are to be in written permission by Natalee Henry and Yevgeniya Calendrillo.

Scripture References are from New American Standard Bible (NASB), and the Tree of Life Version, unless otherwise stated.

This book is a part of the Torah for Children Curriculum. www.torah4children.net

ISBN 978-1-51363723-5

Acknowledgments

Thanks to Ken & Lisa Albin, and our Family and Tribes at Save The Nations for your continued love, support, and encouragement throughout our writing journey.

Special thanks to Kiwi Gomes and Tammie Garcia for editing and proofreading, and all the teachers at Save The Nations who have been serving in the children's ministry teaching this curriculum.

CONTENTS

Torah Portion Titles

1.	B'reisheet - In The Beginning	Page 1
2.	Noah - Comfort, Rest	Page 18
3.	Lech Lecha - Get Yourself Out	Page 34
4.	Vayera - He Appeared	Page 52
5.	Chayei Sarah - The Life of Sarah	Page 72
6.	Toldot - Generation/History	Page 88
7.	Vayetze - He Went Out	Page 105
8.	Vayishlach - He Sent	Page 120
9.	Vayeshev - He Continued Living	Page 134
10.	Mikketz - At The End	Page 149
11.	Vayigash - He Approached	Page 165
12.	Vayechi - He Lived	Page 180

About the Authors	Page 197
About the Book	Page 199
Coming Soon	Page 199

NOTE TO TEACHERS/PARENTS:

Dear Teachers and Parents,

Thank you for choosing to help us equip our children in the Torah Way of the Messiah. We are grateful for you and your time of service.

Each lesson is designed as a guide for teaching the Torah Portions. We encourage you to review the lesson in advance to become familiar with the material provided and allow the Holy Spirit to give you insights for teaching the lesson.

Each lesson is structured so our children will learn from the Torah Portions and see the connection with Yeshua (Jesus), and the work of the Holy Spirit. Our aim is not just to give information but to teach Torah principles and demonstrate how to use them in their lives.

Every lesson has a general summary of the Torah Portion and a lesson discussion. Every lesson has practical applications and questions. The questions are given at the end of the lesson, however, the teacher can incorporate the questions at any time during the lesson. The practical applications are excellent ways for the children to make the connection between Torah and their everyday lives.

Craft Templates are available on our website: www.torah4children.net

Thanks again for your time and service in helping to equip our children in the Torah Way of the Messiah.

SUGGESTED CLASS SCHEDULE

Welcome

Practical Application Follow-up implemented after first lesson *(See the Practical Application Page)*

Torah Portion Lesson

Bathroom Break

Crafts

Snacks

LESSON CONTENTS

Torah Portion Name and meaning
Torah Portion Theme
Torah Portion Outline
Lesson
    Title & Meaning
    Scriptures
    Theme
    Summary
    Lesson Discussion
    Turning Point *(THIS SECTION IS FOR CHILDREN 9 YEARS OLD AND OLDER.)*
Practical Applications
Questions and Answer Sheet
Crafts and Instructions

B'reisheet
"In the Beginning"

Torah Portion 1:
B'reisheet - In the Beginning

Scripture Reading:
Genesis 1:1-6:1, Isaiah 42:5-43:10, John 1:1-17, Psalm 139

B'reisheet is the Hebrew word that means ***"In the Beginning."***
It is the first phrase of our Torah reading in Genesis 1:1.

Genesis 1:1
In the beginning God created the heavens and the earth.

The Theme of the Torah Portion:
The Beginning of All Living Things Created by God.

Genesis 1:1-3
1 In the beginning God created the heavens and the earth. **2** Now the earth was chaos and waste, darkness was on the surface of the deep, and the *Ruach Elohim* (Spirit of the Lord) was hovering upon the surface of the water. **3** Then God said, "Let there be light!" and there was light.

Torah Portion Outline:

Genesis Chapter 1:1-1:31
- The Creation

Genesis Chapter 2:1-3
- Sabbath Rest

Genesis Chapter 2:4-24
- The Garden

Genesis Chapter 3:1-24
- Adam and Eve, and the Serpent

Genesis Chapter 4:1-25
- Cain and Abel

Genesis Chapter 5:1-6:8
- All the Families from Adam and Eve to the Birth of Noah

LESSON SUMMARY:

B'reisheet tells us about the days of creation. God created everything in six days and rested on the seventh day. He planted a beautiful Garden in Eden as a home for Adam and his wife Eve. In the garden, they had every kind of fruit and vegetable to eat.

There were also two special trees. One was called the Tree of Life and the other was called the Tree of Knowledge of Good and Evil. God told them they could eat from every tree but not from the Tree of Knowledge of Good and Evil.

Then things took an unexpected turn. There was an evil serpent in the garden who tricked Eve to eat from the Tree of Good and Evil and she shared it with Adam. The woman and the man were all punished because they listened to the serpent and ate from the tree. The serpent was also punished. Adam and Eve were put out of the garden and had to learn to provide for themselves.

Adam and Eve had two sons; Cain and Abel who were both farmers. Cain was a vegetable farmer and Abel was an animal farmer. One day they brought an offering to God. God accepted Abel's offering but He did not accept Cain's offering because it wasn't the best he had in his garden. Abel gave God the firstborn and best from his animals. Cain was angry and he had a fight with his brother Abel and killed him. Cain was punished for killing his brother Abel.

Genesis 4:3-9
3 So it happened after some time that Cain brought an offering of the fruit of the ground to *Adonai*, **4** while Abel—he also brought of the firstborn of his flock and their fat portions. Now *Adonai* looked favorably upon Abel and his offering, **5** but upon Cain and his offering He did not look favorably. Cain became very angry, and his countenance fell.
6 Then *Adonai* said to Cain, "Why are you angry? And why has your countenance fallen? **7** If you do well, it will lift. But if you do not do well, sin is crouching at the doorway. Its desire is for you, but you must master it." **8** Cain spoke to Abel his brother. While they were in the field, Cain rose up against Abel his brother and killed him. **9** Then *Adonai* said to Cain, "Where is Abel, your brother?" "I don't know," he said. "Am I my brother's keeper?"

Years later after Abel died Eve gave birth to another son, and she named him Seth. She said God has given her another son because she lost her son Abel. People were multiplying on the earth and there were many families. As the families grew larger and larger, people didn't obey God and follow His commands. They did only what made them feel good, but Noah was favored by God because He did what pleased God. There was a man by the name of Lamech who had a son, he named his son Noah because he believed Noah will bring comfort and rest from all the evil and violence that the people were doing. Noah learned the commandments of God and he obey them. Noah found favor with God.

LESSON DISCUSSION:

THE SEVEN DAYS OF CREATION

Day 1 - God created light and darkness. The light He called day, darkness He called night. (Genesis 1:1- 3)

Day 2 - God separated the waters. He created the sky to separate the upper waters from the lower waters on the ground. (Genesis 1:6-10)

Day 3 - Grass, green plants with seeds, fruit trees making fruits all according to their kind. (Genesis 1:11-13)

Day 4 - God created the sun, and moon and starts to separate the day from the night. He placed them in the sky as signs for His seasons, days, and years. (Genesis 1:14-19)

Day 5 - God created all the living water creatures according to their kind and all winged flying creatures *(birds)* according to their kind. He blessed them saying "Be fruitful and multiply and fill the water in the seas. Let the flying creatures multiply on the land."(Genesis 1:20-23)

Day 6 - God created all the animals, crawling creatures, and insects on the land according to their kind and blessed them to be fruitful and multiply. (Genesis 1:24-28)

God also created man on the sixth day. (Genesis 1:26-28)
Then God said, **"Let Us make man in Our image, after Our likeness!** Let them rule over the fish of the sea, over the flying creatures of the sky, over the livestock, over the whole earth, and over every crawling creature that crawls on the land." **27** God created humankind in His image, in the image of God He created him, male and female He created them. **28** God blessed them and God said to them, "Be fruitful and multiply, fill the land, and conquer it. Rule over the fish of the sea, the flying creatures of the sky, and over every animal that crawls on the land."

Day 7 - God rested from all His work. Blessed the seventh day and called it holy. (Genesis 2:1-3)

TURNING POINT:

THINGS TOOK A TURN

Adam and Eve disobeyed God and because of their disobedience, they were put out of the garden. God had to make a way for us to return to the garden to walk and talk with Him. In Genesis 1:14-15 *Adonai Elohim* said to the serpent, "Because you did this (tricked the women), Cursed are you above all the livestock and above every animal of the field. On your belly will you go, and dust will you eat all the days of your life. **15** I will put animosity between you and the woman—**between your seed and her seed. He will crush your head, and you will crush his heel."**

God was speaking of Yeshua who would one day come to earth and live a perfect life, obeying all that God tells Him to say and do. He would die for us so we can return to the garden.

CAN WE RETURN TO THE GARDEN?

We can return to the garden because of Yeshua's obedience to God, and the help of the Holy Spirit (Ruach HaKodesh). When we put our trust in Yeshua as the Son of God, the Father sends the Holy Spirit to teach us how to walk in obedience to His word. One day Yeshua will return to take us back to the garden with Him.

John 1:1-4, 14 (NIV)
1 In the beginning was the Word. The Word was with God, and the Word was God. **2** He was with God in the beginning. **3** All things were made through Him, and apart from Him nothing was made that has come into being. **4** In Him was life, and the life was the light of men. **14** And the Word became flesh and tabernacled among us. We looked upon His glory, the glory of the one and only from the Father, full of grace and truth.

John 3:35-36 (NIV)
35 The Father loves the Son and has placed everything in his hands. **36** Whoever believes in the Son has eternal life, but whoever rejects the Son will not see life, for God's wrath remains on them.

John 14:15-21 (NIV)

15 "If you love me, keep my commands. **16** And I will ask the Father, and he will give you another advocate to help you and be with you forever — **17** the Spirit of truth. The world cannot accept him, because it neither sees him nor knows him. But you know him, for he lives with you and will be in you. **18** I will not leave you as orphans; I will come to you. **19** Before long, the world will not see me anymore, but you will see me. Because I live, you also will live. **20** On that day you will realize that I am in my Father, and you are in me, and I am in you. **21** Whoever has my commands and keeps them is the one who loves me. The one who loves me will be loved by my Father, and I too will love them and show myself to them."

PRACTICAL APPLICATIONS

CHILDREN 4-6 YEARS OLD

1. Obey your parents and teachers.

2. Always be kind to your friends and family even when you are sad or feel angry.

3. Be kind to a classmate who does not have any friends.

CHILDREN 7-12 YEARS OLD

1. The Tree of Life and the Tree of Knowledge of Good and Evil.
Are you obedient to your parents, adults *(those responsible for you when your parents are not around)*, and God's commandments?

Actions: What you do shows which tree you are eating from.

Words: The words you speak will be encouraging and sweet when you eat from the Tree of Life.

2. Cain & Abel:
Do you act like Cain or Abel when you are with your friends or when your parents and teachers tell you something you do not like?

3. Demonstrating God's Love:
How can I use what I learned today to share with my family and friends that God loves us and wants us to obey His commandments?

QUESTIONS - TEACHERS ANSWER KEY

1. What is the name of the Torah Portion?
B'reisheet

2. What is the meaning of the name of the Torah Portion?
A.   End   B. In the Beginning   C. Creation

3. What is the Torah Portion about?
The seven days of Creation, Adam and Eve, the Garden and serpent, Cain and Abel *(Any of these answers or answer given about the story is acceptable)*

4. What did Adam and Eve do, that God told them not to do?
Ate from the Tree of Good and Evil

5. What did God create on day one?
Answer: light and darkness

6. What did God create on day two?
Answer: upper and lower waters

7. What did God create on day three?
Answer: plants, trees with seeds, fruit trees

8. What did God create on day four?
Answer: sun, moon, stars

9. What did God create on day five?
Answer: fish, water creatures, birds

10. What did God create on day six?
Answer: animals and man

11. What did God create on day seven?
Answer: Rest, (sabbath rest)

12. What is the story about in the garden?
God, Adam and Eve, and Serpent

13. What did God create in His image?
Man

14. Where did God put Adam and Eve to live?
Garden of Eden

15. Where did God plant the Tree of Life and the Tree of Good and Evil?
They were in the middle of the Garden

16. What happened when Adam and Eve ate from the Tree of Good and Evil?
Their eyes were opened. They saw their nakedness. They were put out of the Garden of Eden

17. Who was tricked by the serpent?
Eve

18. How can we return to the Garden?
By trusting in Yeshua and obeying God's commandments

19. Who did Yeshua say will help us to obey God's commandments?
The Holy Spirit

20. Which day did God bless and said it is holy?
The seventh day

QUESTIONS - CHILDREN'S COPY

1. What is the name of the Torah Portion?

2. What is the meaning of the name of the Torah Portion?

3. What is the Torah Portion about?

4. What did Adam and Eve do, that God told them not to do?

5. What did God create on day one?

6. What did God create on day two?

7. What did God create on day three?

8. What did God create on day four?

9. What did God create on day five?

10. What did God create on day six?

11. What did God create on day seven?

12. What is the story about in the garden?

13. What did God create in His image?

14. Where did God put Adam and Eve to live?

15. Where did God plant the Tree of Life and the Tree of Good and Evil?

16. What happened when Adam and Eve ate from the Tree of Good and Evil?

17. Who was tricked by the serpent?

18. How can we return to the Garden?

19. Who did Yeshua say will help us to obey God's commandments?

20. Which day did God bless and said it is holy?

CRAFTS FOR TORAH PORTION B'REISHEET

SUPPLIES:

1. Construction paper of various colors
2. White plain paper
3. Colored pencils or markers
4. Scissors
5. Glue/Glue Sticks
6. Print-outs
7. Stickers of plants/trees, birds/animals/fish Could be found on Amazon
8. Cotton balls
9. White pencils or pens

We will be creating artwork for each of the seven days of Creations!

DAY 1 - Draw Light with a white pencil or pen on black construction paper. Mark it as Day 1 anywhere on a page. This could be done in various creative ways. The idea is shown.

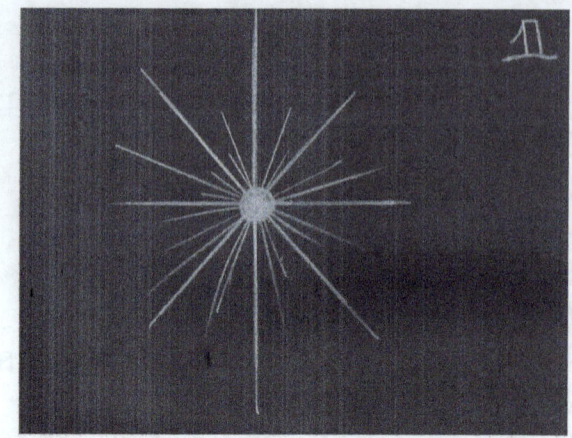

DAY 2 - Draw the water and the sky. For young children, pre-draw it so they could color it. For older children - allow them to draw it themselves. Color it. Put cotton balls as clouds. Mark it as Day 2 anywhere on a page.

DAY 3 - Pre-drawn the land and the sea. Children cut out a drawing of a palm tree and put it on paper. Color everything. Mark it as Day 3 and mark it as Good!

DAY 4 - Cut out black and white planets and stars. Color it and paste it on dark-color construction paper. Mark it as Day 4 and mark it as Good!

DAY 5 - Pre-drawn ocean and sky. Have the children color it. Mark it as day 5 and mark it as Good!

DAY 6 - cut out a drawing of Adam and Eve and place it anywhere on the bottom of the page. Pages are already pre-drawn with trees and plants. Have the children color all and mark it as Day 6.

DAY 7 - Have children cut out the drawing of the planet and paste it on Yellow Construction paper. Have them creatively write on a paper that God's work was done and it was a SABBATH DAY! A day of Holiness and Rest!

STICKERS ASSIGNMENT

The children should have time to take the stickers mentioned in the supplies and place them properly.

Plants on days 3 and 6. Fish on Day 5. Birds on Day 5 and 6. Animals/insects/reptiles on Day 6.

We want the children to be able to finish all 7 days, so no more than 6-8 minutes per each day of creation.

If they didn't finish something, they could finish it at home, but we want them to be able to work on each day and have time for stickers. And if the sermon goes longer, they could come back and work on what they didn't finish.

Noach
"Comfort and Rest"

Portion 2:

Noah - Comfort, Rest

Scriptures: Genesis 6:9-11:32, Isaiah 54:1–55:5, Psalm 29, Luke 17:20-27, Matthew 24:36-44, Acts 2:1-16

Noah is from the Hebrew word Noach which means **"Comfort"**, or **"Rest"**. It is found in Genesis 5:29 of our Torah reading.

Genesis 5:28-29 (TLV)

And Lamech lived a hundred eighty and two years, and begat a son: **29** And he called his name Noah, saying, This *same* shall comfort us concerning our work and toil of our hands, because of the ground which the LORD hath cursed.

The Theme of The Torah Portion:
A Covenant of Love and Obedience

Genesis 7:1-4, Genesis 9:8-16

Noah was obedient to God. He was considered righteous because he was obedient. God loved him and his family and saved them in the ark. He made a covenant with Noah and all living creatures to never again destroy them from the earth with water. He gave the rainbow as a sign of his covenant.

Genesis 7:1-4 Then *Adonai* said to Noah, "Come—you and all your household—into the ark. For you only do I perceive as righteous before Me in this generation. **2** Of every clean animal you shall take with you seven of each kind, male and female; and of the animals which themselves are not clean two, male and female; **3** also of the flying creatures of the sky seven of every kind, male and female, to keep offspring alive on the face of the whole land. **4** For in seven more days, I am going to make it rain upon the land forty days and forty nights, and I will wipe out all existence that I made from the face of the ground. **5** So Noah did all just as *Adonai* commanded him.

Genesis 9:8-16
Then God said to Noah and to his sons with him, saying, **9** "Now I, behold, I am about to establish My covenant with you, and with your seed after you, **10** and with every living creature that is with you, including the flying creatures, the livestock, and every wild animal with you, of all that is coming out of the ark—every animal of the earth. **11** I will confirm My covenant with you—never again will all flesh be cut off by the waters of the flood, and never again will there be a flood to ruin the land." **12** Then God said, "This is the sign of the covenant that I am making between Me and you, and every living creature that is with you for all future generations. **13** My rainbow do I place in the cloud, and it will be a sign of the covenant between Me and the land. **14** Whenever I bring clouds over the land and the rainbow appears in the clouds, **15** I will remember My covenant that is

between Me and you and every living creature of all flesh. Never again will the waters become a flood to destroy all flesh. **16** When the rainbow is in the cloud, I will look at it, to remember the perpetual covenant between God and every living creature of all flesh that is on the land."

Torah Portion Outline

Genesis 6:9-21
- The Ark

Genesis 7:1-8:14
- The Great Flood

Genesis 8:15-22
- Noah Offers a Sacrifice

Genesis 9:1-17
- God's Covenant Promise

Genesis 9:18-10:32
- Noah's Family Tree

Genesis 11:1-9
- The Tower of Babel

Genesis 11:10-32
- Where did Abram (Abraham) come From?

LESSON SUMMARY:

Mankind became very corrupt on earth doing whatever pleased them. It made God angry and He decided to destroy the earth and all living things. Noah was a righteous man, he did and said things that pleased God. Noah had three sons; Shem, Ham, and Japheth. Genesis 6:13-21.

God told Noah to build an ark. He gave Noah all the measurements for building the ark and also told him what type of material to use. God also gave Noah instructions for all the animals he should take with him in the ark. Noah built the ark and did everything just as God told him. After Noah had finished building the ark, God told him to go into the ark with his family and take the animals, because He would cause it to rain in the next seven days. Noah and his family went into the ark and so did all the animals, birds, and insects. He took two pairs of each unclean animal but seven pairs of each clean animal. God shut the door of the ark. Then He made it rain for forty (40) days and forty (40) nights.

God made a covenant with Noah not to use a flood ever again for punishment and gave him the rainbow as a sign of His covenant promise. Noah's sons and their wives began to have children. Years later when there were once again numerous people on the earth, they forgot about God and started doing things their way. This time they decided to build a tower to reach the heavens where God dwells. God did not want mankind to build a tower to heaven. All the people spoke the same language so He (God) caused them to speak different languages and they could no longer understand each other, so the tower was named the Tower of Babel.

Noah's son Shem did what was right in God's eyes just as his father did. He taught his children to obey God's commandments. Many years after Shem died, Abram was born. Abram also obeyed God's commandments and lived his life to please God.

LESSON DISCUSSION:

THE GREAT FLOOD

Genesis 7:1-5, 13 & 17-18 (TLV)

Then *Adonai* said to Noah, "Come—you and all your household—into the ark. For you only do I perceive as righteous before Me in this generation. **2** Of every clean animal you shall take with you seven of each kind, male and female; and of the animals which themselves are not clean two, male and female; **3** also of the flying creatures of the sky seven of every kind, male and female, to keep offspring alive on the face of the whole land. **4** For in seven more days, I am going to make it rain upon the land forty days and forty nights, and I will wipe out all existence that I made from the face of the ground. **5** So Noah did all just as *Adonai* commanded him. **13** On that same day Noah, along with Noah's sons Shem, Ham and Japheth, Noah's wife and the three wives of Noah's sons with them, entered the ark, **17** The flood was forty days upon the land, and the waters increased and lifted the ark, so that it rose above the land. **18** The waters overpowered and became very mighty over the land, and the ark drifted on the surface of the water.

Water covered all the lands of the earth, even the highest mountains were covered. Everything on dry land died; and also all the birds of the air. Only eight people were saved from the great flood; Noah, his family, and all the animals that were in the ark with them.

God remembered Noah and all the animals that were in the ark, so he caused a wind to pass over the land to make the water go down. The ark rested on the mountains of Ararat in the seventh month, on the seventh day. Noah wanted to know if it was safe to go outside so he sent a dove through the window, but the dove returned because it could not find a tree to live in. Seven days later he sent the dove out again, this time the dove returned with an olive leaf in its mouth. That was a sign to Noah that the flood waters were going down. He waited seven more days, then sent the dove out again. This time the dove did not return. Noah knew then that it was safe for him and his family and all the animals to leave the ark. God told Noah to come out of the ark. They lived in the ark for three hundred and seventy-five fifty (375) days. Noah was grateful that he and his family survived the great flood so Noah built an altar and offered a sacrifice to God and gave Him thanks for saving him and his family.

Genesis 8:6-11 (TLV)

6 It was at the end of forty days that Noah opened the window of the ark that he had made. **7** Then he sent out a raven and it kept going back and forth until the waters were drying up from the land. **8** Then he sent out a dove to see whether the waters had receded from the surface of the ground. **9** But the dove did not find a resting place for the sole of her foot. She returned to him in the ark because water covered the surface of the whole land. He stretched out his hand and he took her, and brought her to him into the ark. **10** So he waited yet another seven days and again he sent the dove out from the ark. **11** The dove came to him at evening, and surprisingly—a freshly plucked olive leaf was in its mouth. So Noah knew that the waters had receded from the land. **12** After he waited seven more days, he sent out the dove, but she did not return to him again.

TURNING POINT:

GOD'S COVENANT

God blessed Noah and his family with the same blessing He gave to Adam and Eve when He created them. He said to them; "Be fruitful and multiply and fill the land." Genesis 9.

God also gave them rule over everything on the earth. He told them they could eat meat from all the clean animals but to make sure they did not eat the blood from the animals because life is in the blood.

When God saw all the dead animals and people, he was sorrowful. He promised never again to destroy mankind by water. He made a covenant with all living things; mankind and animals. This covenant was for Noah and his sons and all future generations. This includes you and me. God told Noah that He will put a rainbow in the clouds whenever it rained as a sign that He (God) is keeping His promise never to destroy all life on earth with a great flood.

Genesis 9:8-11 (TLV)
Then God said to Noah and to his sons with him, saying, **9** "Now I, behold, I am about to establish My covenant with you, and with your seed after you, **10** and with every living creature that is with you, including the flying creatures, the livestock, and every wild animal with you, of all that is coming out of the ark—every animal of the earth. **11** I will confirm My covenant with you—never again will all flesh be cut off by the waters of the flood, and never again will there be a flood to ruin the land."

GOD'S PROMISE TO US
The promise God made to Noah is also a promise He made to us. In the ark, Noah and His family were saved from the flood. They did not die because Noah was obedient to God. He built the ark just as God told him to build it. He took all the animals God told him to take. He went into the ark with his family on the day God told him to go in it. God promises to protect us and keep us safe if we obey Him. When we put our hope and

trust in Yeshua, He delivers us from the consequences of death. God also gives us the Holy Spirit to be our comforter.

John 3:16 (TLV)

"For God so loved the world that He gave His one and only Son, that whoever believes in Him shall not perish but have eternal life."

Just like Noah sent the dove out to make sure it was safe to leave the ark, we have the Holy Spirit to let us know if the places we want to go are safe or not. We have a promise of eternal life with Yeshua, but we must be obedient and not be like the people who lived in the days of Noah. They did not listen to Noah or obey God's word. If you want to live forever with Yeshua you must love and obey His commandments.

Matthew 3:13-17 (TLV)

Then *Yeshua* came from Galilee to John, to be immersed by him in the Jordan. **14** But John tried to prevent Him, saying, "I need to be immersed by You, and You are coming to me?" **15** But *Yeshua* responded, "Let it happen now, for in this way it is fitting for us to fulfill all righteousness." So John yielded to Him. **16** After being immersed, *Yeshua* rose up out of the water; and behold, the heavens were opened to Him, and He saw the *Ruach Elohim* descending like a dove and coming upon Him. **17** And behold, a voice from the heavens said, "This is My Son, whom I love; with Him I am well pleased!"

PRACTICAL APPLICATIONS

FOR CHILDREN 4-6 YEARS OLD
Think of ways to be more obedient to your parents this week. *(Teacher can also share any idea that comes to mind).*

Examples:
1. Putting away your toys when you are told to do so.
2. Helping Mom and Dad keep your room clean.

Ask the Holy Spirit to help you hear the voice of God.

FOR CHILDREN 7-12 YEARS OLD
Make note of your actions every day for the next seven (7) days. Would God consider those actions righteous and pleasing to Him?

Write down two conversations you had with a friend or family member. Would you be able to have those conversations with God?

Ask the Holy Spirit to help you hear the voice of God.

FOLLOW-UP FROM THE LAST TORAH PORTION
Ask who wants to share from last week's practical application

CHILDREN 4-6 YEARS OLD

1. Obey your parents and teachers.

2. Always be kind to your friends and family even when you are sad.

3. Be kind to someone who does not have any friends.

CHILDREN 7-12 YEARS OLD

1. The Tree of Life and the Tree of Knowledge of Good and Evil.

Are you obedient to your parents, adults *(those responsible for you when your parents are not around)*, and God's commandments?

Actions: What you do shows which tree you are eating from

Words: The words you speak will be encouraging and sweet when you eat from the Tree of Life

2. Cain & Abel:
Do you act like Cain or Abel when you are with your friends or when your parents and teachers tell you something you do not like?

3. Demonstrating God's Love:
How can I use what I learned today to share with my family and friends that God loves us and wants us to obey His commandments?

QUESTIONS - TEACHERS ANSWER KEY

1. **How many people were in the ark?**
   Eight (8) people

2. **How long did it rain?**
   Forty (40) days and forty (40) nights

3. **Who shut the Ark's door?**
   God

4. **What kind of bird did Noah send out to see if it was safe to leave the ark?**
   Dove and Raven

5. **How long did Noah wait before sending the dove out the second time?**
   Seven days

6. **What did Noah do when he came out of the ark?**
   Built an altar and offered sacrifice to God

7. **On what Mountains did the ark rest after the flood?**
   Mountains of Ararat

8. **What was the sign of the covenant God made with Noah?**
   Rainbow

9. **Why was Noah favored by God?**
   He was obedient to God and he did what was right.

10. **How did Noah know it was safe to leave the ark?**
    The dove did not return

11. **How many times did Noah send out the dove?**
    Three times

12. **What is the meaning of Noah's name?**
    "Comforter or rest"

13. **Who is our comforter?**
    The Holy Spirit

14. **Share one thing you learned from this lesson.**

QUESTIONS - CHILDREN'S COPY

1. How many people were in the ark?

2. How long did it rain?

3. Who shut the Ark door?

4. What kind of bird did Noah send out to see if it was safe to leave the ark?

5. How long did Noah wait before sending the dove out the second time?

6. What did Noah do when he came out of the ark?

7. On what Mountains did the ark rest after the flood?

8. What was the sign of the covenant God made with Noah?

9. Why was Noah favored by God?

10. How did Noah know it was safe to leave the ark?

11. How many times did Noah send out the dove?

12. What is the meaning of Noah's name?

13. Who is our comforter?

14. Share one thing you learned from this lesson.

CRAFTS FOR TORAH PORTION NOACH

SUPPLIES:
Brown Construction Paper
Popsicle Sticks
Animal Stickers
Cardstock Paper
Sequins of Rainbow Colors and Black
Glue/Glue Sticks
Markers/Pencils
Scissors
Small Leaves To Imitate Olive Branch

1. **NOAH'S ARK ACTIVITY**.

Pre-cut the shape of an ark from brown construction paper. Glue it to card stock, to make it thicker. Glue popsicle sticks as shown. Color a few of them brown for design. Paste various animals in empty spots.

2. **GOD'S RAINBOW ACTIVITY**.

Color the pre-drawn rainbow in the correct colors and decorate it with sequins! Inside the rainbow, write out the colors of the rainbow and then write who God is corresponding to the first letter of each color. **Example:** Red - Righteousness.

3. **DOVE WITH AN OLIVE BRANCH**

Cut out from card stock the dove. Place a black sequin as an eye. Glue the popsicle stick to the bottom. Take a little leaf and paste it where the mouth is.

Lech Lecha
"Get Yourself Out"

Torah Portion 3:
Lech Lecha - Get Yourself Out

Scriptures:
Genesis 12:1-17:27, Isaiah 40:27-41:16,
Psalm 110, John 8:51-58

Lech Lecha is the Hebrew phrase translated as **"get yourself out."** It is found in the first verse of our Torah Portion.

Genesis 12:1 (Complete Jewish Bible)
Now *Adonai* said to Avram (Abram), **"Get yourself out** of your country, away from your kinsmen and away from your father's house, and go to the land that I will show you.

The Theme of the Torah Portion:

Obedience

Genesis 12:1-5 Complete Jewish Bible (CJB)

Now *Adonai* said to Avram (Abram), "Get yourself out of your country, away from your kinsmen and away from your father's house, and go to the land that I will show you. **2** I will make of you a great nation, I will bless you, and I will make your name great; and you are to be a blessing. **3** I will bless those who bless you, but I will curse anyone who curses you; and by you all the families of the earth will be blessed." **4** So Avram went, as *Adonai* had said to him, and Lot went with him. Avram was 75 years old when he left Haran. **5** Avram took his wife Sarai, his brother's son Lot, and all their possessions which they had accumulated, as well as the people they had acquired in Haran; then they set out for the land of Kena'an and entered the land of Kena'an.

Torah Portion Outline

Genesis Chapter 12
- God Calls Abram

Genesis Chapter 13
- Lot and Abram Shepherds are Fighting

Genesis Chapter 14
- Abram Rescues Lot, **Genesis 14:1-16**
- Abram Pays Tithes to Melchizedek King of Salem, **Genesis 14:17-24**

Genesis Chapter 15
- God Made a Covenant With Abram

Genesis Chapter 16
- Hagar and Ismael

Genesis Chapter 17
- God Reminds Abram of His Covenant, **Gen.17:**
- The Child of the Promise, **Gen.17:**
- Changed Abram and Sarai's Name, **Gen.17:**
- Covenant Sign of Circumcision, **Gen.17:**

LESSON SUMMARY

God called Abram to leave his family and father's house. He obeyed and left. He took his wife Sarai, his servants, and everything he owned. His nephew Lot also went with him. He went to Canaan and lived in a city called Shechem. He built a tent near a big tree in Moreh.

There was a famine and Abram could not find food, so he decided to go to Egypt for a while before returning to Canaan. Abram and Lot were blessed by God. They had great wealth and many cattle. They had so many cattle that there was not enough grass for both their cattle to eat in the same field. Their shepherds were fighting to feed the cattle. Abram did not want them to fight so he told Lot, it would be best if we don't live in the same place. Choose where you want to live and I will go in the opposite direction. Lot looked and he saw the beautiful fields of Sodom and Gomorrah so he chose to go live there.

Years later after Lot left, the kings of Sodom and Gomorrah were at war with other kings. The kings of Sodom and Gomorrah were afraid and ran to escape into the nearby mountains. The other kings captured all the people of Sodom and Gomorrah and all their possessions. Lot, Abram's nephew, was taken captive. One of the men escaped and went to tell Abram what happened. When Abram heard about Lot, he gave weapons to 318 of his men-servants and they went to fight against the kings who captured Lot. God gave them victory over all the kings and their armies. They brought back Lot and all the people and all their possessions.

Now when Melchizedek King of Salem heard that God gave Abram victory over all the kings he came to meet Abram. He also brought him bread and wine and blessed Abram. Abram gave a tenth of all he owned to Melchizedek as a tithe. The King of Sodom wanted all the people for himself that Abram rescued (Gen.14:21). He said to Abram, give me the people and take the possessions for yourself. Abram told him I will not take anything from you, I only trust God to provide for me.

Sometime later God spoke to Abram in a vision and said to him. Don't be afraid Abram I am your protector and your reward will be great. Abram asked God, what good will Your gift be to me since I have no children and my servant Eliezer of Damascus will inherit all that I own? God spoke to him again and said Eliezer will not inherit your rewards. You will father a child. Go outside. Look at the sky and count the stars if you can. Your descendants will be that many. Abram believed God's words. Because he believed God, God considered him a righteous man. God said to Abram, I am Your God who brought you up out of Ur, to give you this land to be your possession. Abram asked how will I know I will possess it? God told Abram to bring Him a sacrifice offering. Birds of prey were trying to eat the sacrifice but Abram drove them away. Right before sunset, Abram fell asleep and he had a very terrifying dream. God told him in the dream your descendants will be foreigners in a land that is not theirs, and they will be slaves for 430 years. But I will judge that nation, then they will leave with great wealth. After sunset, God made a covenant with Abram. Genesis 15:18-21. He promised that Abram will become a father and Sarai will give birth to a son and his descendants will inherit the land of Canaan.

Ten years after God promised Abram would have a child Sarai still could not get pregnant, so she told Abram to marry her servant, Hagar and maybe she will have a child for him. Abram married Hagar and she became pregnant, but that was not God's plan for them. Hagar no longer wanted to obey Sarai. She acted as if she was better than Sarai because she could have a child and Sarai could not. Sarai was angry with Hagar and treated her unkindly. Hagar ran away because she didn't like the way Sarai treated her. God sent an angel to speak to Hagar and he convinced her to go back home. He told her God will take care of her and her son. Hagar had a son and she named him Ishmael, just as the angel said. Abram was 86 years old when Ishmael was born.

Thirteen years later God reminded Abram and Sarai of the promise He made to them. Sarai would give birth to a son who will be called Isaac. God changed Abram's name to Abraham, father of nations, and Sarai's name He changed to Sarah which means princess. God gave Abraham a sign as a reminder of His covenant with him. He told Abraham to circumcise every male in his house, and in the future when a son is born he must be circumcised eight days after he is born.

LESSON DISCUSSION:

THE CALL: ABRAM WALKS IN OBEDIENCE

It was years after the great flood that God was looking for someone to teach the people how to live in obedience to Him, so God chose Abram. God called Abram and told him to leave his family and go to a land where He would show him.

Genesis 12:1-4 (CJB)

Now *Adonai* said to Avram (Abram), "Get yourself out of your country, away from your kinsmen and away from your father's house, and go to the land that I will show you. **2** I will make of you a great nation, I will bless you, and I will make your name great; and you are to be a blessing. **3** I will bless those who bless you, but I will curse anyone who curses you; and by you all the families of the earth will be blessed." **4** So Avram (Abram) went, as *Adonai* had said to him, and Lot went with him. Avram was 75 years old when he left Haran."

Abram did not know where God was sending him, but he was obedient and left. Abram was obedient but there was a problem, his nephew Lot decided to go with him. While on their journey, Abram had to tell Lot it was not good for them to live together because the servants who took care of their flock were fighting to feed the animals. Lot went to live in the city of Sodom because it looked beautiful and reminded him of the Garden of Eden.

When God tells us to do something we must be careful not to carry along with us someone who does not understand God's mission for us, because they will cause trouble for us.

God visited Abram after Lot left. This time he said to him, *"lift up your eyes, now, and look from the place where you are, to the north, south, east and west. For all the land that you are looking at, I will give to you and to your seed forever. I will make your seed like the dust of the earth so that if one could count the dust of the earth, then your seed could also be counted. Get up! Walk about the land through its length and width—for I will give it to you."* **Genesis 13:15-17**

God appeared to Abram in a vision and reminded him of His promise. The only thing Abram needed to do was to remain obedient. God told Abram not to be afraid because 'I am your shield and your reward is very great', Genesis 15:1. Abram said to God 'what good is your reward since You promised that I will have many children and my wife Sarai still cannot get pregnant?' What will you give me so I know this will happen?

God promised that Abram's children would be as many as the stars of the sky and the sand of the sea, but Abram and Sarai did not have any children. How could this be Abram thought?

Genesis 15: 5-9 (TLV)

He took him outside and said, "Look up now, at the sky, and count the stars—if you are able to count them." Then He said to him, "So shall your seed be." **6** Then he believed in *Adonai* and He reckoned it to him as righteousness. **7** Then He said to him, "I am *Adonai* who brought you out from Ur of the Chaldeans, in order to give you this land to inherit it." **8** So he said, "My Lord *Adonai*, how will I know that I will inherit it?" **9** Then He said to him, "Bring Me a three year old young cow, a three year old she-goat, a three year old ram, a turtle-dove and a young bird." **10** So he brought all these to Him and cut them in half, and put each piece opposite the other; but he did not cut the birds."

God also promised that His children and their children will inherit the land that He gave him. **Genesis 15:18,** "*On that day Adonai cut a covenant with Abram, saying, "I give this land to your seed, from the river of Egypt to the great river, the Euphrates River:"*

GOD'S COVENANT AND THE HEIR OF THE PROMISE

When Ismael was thirteen (13) years old, God appeared to Abram again. Abram was now 99 years old, God said to him; *"I am El Shaddai. Continually walk before Me and you will be blameless. My heart's desire is to make My covenant between Me and you, and then I will multiply you exceedingly much."* Genesis 17:1-2

God talked with Abram and said, My covenant promise for you, I will make you a father of many nations. I am also changing your name from Abram to Abraham for you are now the father of many nations. He also changed Sarai's name to Sarah. I will bless her, and she will give birth to a son. She will be a mother of many nations. Abraham laughed when God told him that Sarah will have a son because he was almost 100 years old and Sarah was 90 years old. He said to God, "Let Ismael inherit the land you promised me", but God told him no. Ishmael will not inherit the land, Sarah will have a son and you should call him Isaac.

God gave Abraham a sign as a reminder of His covenant with him. He told Abraham to circumcise every male in his house, and in the future when a son is born he must be circumcised eight days after he is born.

Genesis 17:23 *Then Abraham took Ishmael his son, and all the servants who were born in his house and all who were bought with his money, every male among the men of Abraham's household, and circumcised the flesh of their foreskin in the very same day, as God had said to him.*

Abraham obediently did everything that God told him to do, even when he did not understand why he had to do it.

In this Torah Portion, we see a pattern of obedience. Every person mentioned had a choice whether to obey or not.
- Abram obeyed God
- Sarai obeyed Abram
- Pharaoh obeyed God
- Lot obeyed Abram
- Abram's servant obeyed him
- Hagar obeyed the angel

We too have a choice whether to obey the word of God and our parents. The fifth commandment tells us to honor our Father and Mother so that we may live long. Sometimes it is hard for us to do what God or our parents tell us to do but remember we have a Helper. Last week we learned that God gives us the Ruach HaKodesh (The Holy Spirit) to be our Helper, comforter, and teacher.

John 14:26 *But the Helper, the Holy Spirit, whom the Father will send in My name, He will teach you all things, and bring to your remembrance all that I said to you.*

Yeshua was also obedient to God, His heavenly Father, and his earthly parents.

John 5:19-20 (NASB) Therefore Jesus answered and was saying to them, *"Truly, truly, I say to you, the Son can do nothing of Himself, unless it is something He sees the Father doing; for whatever the Father does, these things the Son also does in like manner.*

For reference

Yeshua and his parents, Mary and Joseph, went to Jerusalem for Passover. On the way back home they realized Yeshua was not with them. They went back to Jerusalem and found him in the temple speaking with the teachers. He said to them, *"Why is it that you were looking for Me? Did you not know that I had to be in My Father's house?"* **50** *But they did not understand the statement which He had made to them.* **51** *And He went down with them and came to Nazareth, and He continued in subjection to them; and His mother treasured all these things in her heart.* **Luke 2:49-52 (NASB)**

Today if you find it hard to be obedient, let us pray and ask the Holy Spirit to help you.

The teacher leads the children into prayer.

TURNING POINT:

WHAT WENT WRONG

Ten years later after God told Abram that he would have children, his wife Sarai still couldn't get pregnant. Sarai said to Abram, take my servant Hagar and marry her, maybe God will cause her to give you a child to fulfill His promise. Abram obeyed Sarai and he married Hagar. Shortly after Hagar got pregnant. Now that Hagar was carrying Abram's child she thought she was better than Sarai and she made fun of Sarai. Sarai did not like the way Hagar was acting, and out of anger Sarai treated, Hagar badly.

Hagar, tired of the way Sarai treated her, decided to run away. God sent an angel to talk with her and convinced her to go back home. Hagar obeyed the angel and went back home. She gave birth to a son and named him Ismael just as the angel of God told her.

Genesis 16:9-11 (TLV)

The angel of *Adonai* said, "Return to your mistress and humble yourself under her hand." **10** Then the angel of *Adonai* said to her, "I will bountifully multiply your seed, and they will be too many to count." **11** Then the angel of *Adonai* said to her, Behold, you are pregnant and about to bear a son, and you shall name him Ishmael— for *Adonai* has heard your affliction.

Abram's family was in trouble because they thought that God forgot about His promise to give them children. They decided to help God. Did God need their help?

When we try to accomplish God's promise the way we think it should happen, or when we think it should happen, we put ourselves in trouble.

When God makes a promise to us He will do it. We just need to be patient and wait for Him to do it His way.

PRACTICAL APPLICATIONS

FOR CHILDREN 4-6 YEARS OLD
- Learn the first commandment with your parents. Exodus 20: 2
- Ask your parents to pray with you every night to hear God's voice.

FOR CHILDREN 7-12 YEARS OLD
- Learn the 1st and 5th Commandments. Exodus 20: 2 & 12

- Ask a close friend to let you know when you are not obedient to your teachers at school or other adults that give you right and Godly instructions.

- Ask the Holy Spirit to help you to hear God's voice and to be obedient even when it is hard.

FOLLOW-UP FROM THE LAST TORAH PORTION
Ask who wants to share from last week's practical application.

FOR CHILDREN 4-6 YEARS OLD
Think of ways to be more obedient to your parents this week. *(Teacher can also share any idea that comes to mind).*

Examples:
1. Putting away your toys when you are told to do so.
2. Helping Mom and Dad keep your room clean.

Ask the Holy Spirit to help you hear the voice of God.

FOR CHILDREN 7-12 YEARS OLD
Make note of your actions every day for the next seven (7) days. Would God consider those actions righteous and pleasing to Him?

Write down two conversations you had with a friend or family member. Would you be able to have those conversations with God?

Ask the Holy Spirit to help you hear the voice of God.

QUESTIONS - TEACHERS ANSWER KEY

1. **What was the first promise God gave Abram?**
   I will make you a great nation

2. **What is the name of the city God told Abram to go to?**
   He did not say.

3. **How old was Abram when God called him?**
   75 years old

4. **Who did Abram pay tithes to?**
   Melchizedek

5. **How many men did Abram go with to rescue Lot?**
   318 men

6. **Where did Lot choose to live?**
   Sodom and Gomorrah

7. **Why were the shepherds of Abram and Lot fighting?**
   The cattle (sheep, animals) were too many to feed in the same field

8. **Why is it important to obey God's command?**
   (Answers may vary based on children's understanding)

9. **What was the name of Sarai's servant that Abram marries?**
   Hagar

10. **What was the name of Abram's first son?**
    Ishmael

11. **What was the sign of God's covenant promise to Abraham?**
    Circumcision

12. Who was the child God promised?
   Isaac

13. How old was Abraham when he was circumcised?
   99 years old

QUESTIONS - CHILDREN'S COPY

1. What was the first promise God gave Abram?

2. What is the name of the city God told Abram to go to?

3. How old was Abram when God called him?

4. Who did Abram pay tithes to?

5. How many men did Abram go with to rescue Lot?

6. Where did Lot choose to live?

7. Why were the shepherds of Abram and Lot fighting?

8. Why is it important to obey God's command?

9. What was the name of Sarai's servant that Abram marries?

10. What was the name of Abram's first son?

11. What was the sign of God's covenant promise to Abraham?

12. Who was the child God promised?

13. How old was Abraham when he was circumcised?

CRAFT FOR TORAH PORTION LECH LECHA

SUPPLIES
*12"x12" black cardstock
Gold cardstock
White cardstock
Black/brown construction paper
Gold/silver stars stickers
Glitter
Color sequins
Markers/pencils
White pencil
Beige/light color pencils
Glue

1 "LOOK AT THE SKY" ACTIVITY.

Glue pre-cut pieces of gold cardstock at the bottom of the black cardstock paper.

Color the pre-drawn picture of Abraham, cut it out, and glue it on the left-hand side of the black cardstock.

Color the pre-drawn picture of the camel, cut it out, and glue it on the right-hand side of the black cardstock. Decorate the camel's saddle with sequins.

Place Gold and silver star stickers all over the black cardstock to represent the starry sky.

Put little glue dots in various spots of the black cardstock and sprinkle glitter on it to create glitter dots. Take white a pencil and draw rays of light as shown.

THE FINISHED WORK

2 Abraham's Footsteps Activity

Teach children how to draw Footprints with light pencils on black or brown construction paper.

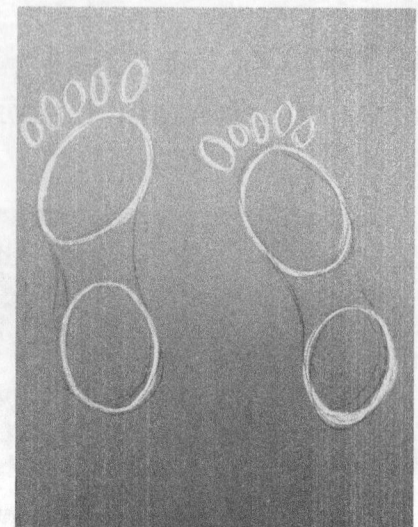 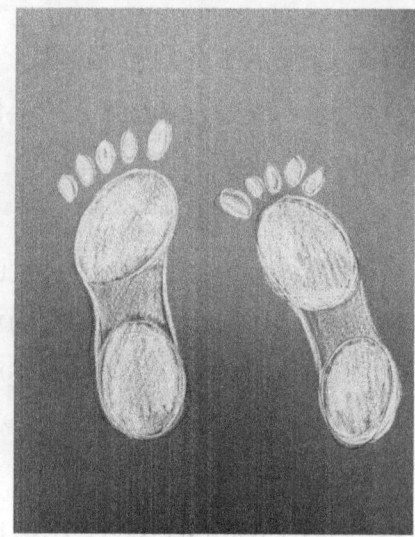

Vayera
"He Appeared"

Torah Portion 4:
Vayera - He Appeared

Scriptures: Genesis 18:1–22:24,
2 Kings 4:1–37, Psalm 11, Luke 17: 28-37

Vayera is Hebrew for "He Appeared." It is found in the first verse of our Torah Portion.

Genesis 18:1 *Then **Adonai appeared** to him at Mamre's large trees while he was sitting in the entrance of his tent during the heat of the day.*

The theme of the Torah Portion:
Pleasing To God

Genesis 22:15-18 TLV

15 Then the angel of the Lord called to Abraham a second time from heaven, **16** and said, "By Myself I have sworn, declares the Lord, because you have done this thing and have not withheld your son, your only son, **17** indeed I will greatly bless you, and I will greatly multiply your seed as the stars of the heavens and as the sand which is on the seashore; and your seed shall possess the gate of their enemies. **18** In your seed all the nations of the earth shall be blessed, because you have obeyed My voice."

Torah Portion Outline

Genesis Chapter 18
- The Promised Child, Isaac

Genesis 19
- Sodom and Gomorrah Destroyed

Genesis 20
- Abraham Lied to King Abimelech

Genesis 21
- Isaac is Born, **Genesis 21:1-21**
- Abraham's Covenant with King Abimelech, **Genesis 21:22-34**

Genesis 22
- The Offering: Isaac and The Ram

TORAH PORTION SUMMARY (FOR TEACHERS ONLY)

One afternoon after Abraham was circumcised he was sitting at the door of his tent by a big tree. He looked up and saw three men who were angels standing a distance away from him. He got up and ran to the men and invited them to come and visit so they could rest and get something to eat. They agreed to go with him. Abraham ran to his tent and asked Sarah to make three cakes for the men. Then He went to his herd of animals and got the best calf he could find and gave it to his servant and told him to cook it for the three men. The men were sitting under the big three. Abraham took the cakes, the meat that was cooked, and some milk and gave the meal to them to eat.

When they finished eating the angels asked Abraham, where is Sarah, your wife? He told them she was in the tent. They said to him, next year this time we will return and Sarah will have a son. Sarah heard what the man said and she laughed. Sarah and Abraham were very old. Sarah was too old to have a child. They told Abraham nothing is too hard for the Lord. Sarah will give birth to a son at the appointed time.

Two of the men left and went toward Sodom and Gomorrah. They were sent by God to destroy the city because the people were ungodly. The people of Sodom and Gomorrah were doing things that pleased themselves and not what pleased God. One of the men stayed with Abraham. Abraham said to the one who was with him, will the Lord really destroy the righteous with the wicked? Abraham said to him; what if there are fifty righteous people, will God still destroy the city. Abraham knew that God is righteous and a God who is just. He would not punish the righteous with the wicked. God said, if I find fifty who are doing what pleases Me, I will not destroy the city because of them. Abraham did not want God to destroy the city so he asked, what if there are only forty-five, or thirty, or twenty, or only ten people who are doing what please You? God said to him, if I find ten in the city that are righteous (who do things that please Me), I will not destroy the city because of them. God did not find anyone in the city that pleased Him, except for Lot and his family. He told the two men who went to Sodom and Gomorrah to destroy the city but make sure Lot and his family left before they destroy it. Lot and his wife, and two daughters were taken out of the city by the two men. They told them not to look back. Lot's wife did not obey and she looked back while they were leaving and she became a pillar of salt. God caused fire to fall from heaven and burned up the city. Lot and his daughters went to live in a city called Zoar.

After seeing what God did to the city of Sodom and Gomorrah, Abraham went to live in the city of Gerar. Abraham said to Sarah, tell everyone you are my sister as we did in Egypt. When Abimelech, king of Gerar, saw how beautiful Sarah was he took her to his house. God spoke to the king in a dream and said to him you are a dead man because you have taken another man's wife to be your wife. Abimelech answered God, they told me she was his sister and that's why I took her. God replied, yes I know, that is why I did not allow you to touch her. Give her back to her husband and you will live. In the morning Abimelech took Sarah to Abraham. He asked Abraham, why did you lie to me and cause a great sin to come on me and my Kingdom? Abraham answered, I was afraid, I didn't know if the people have respect and honor for God. Abimelech blessed Abraham and Sarah, gave them gifts, and sent them away.

God remembered the promise He made to Sarah. She became pregnant and gave birth to a son at the time the angel said she would. She named him Isaac, which means laughter. When Isaac was eight days old, Abraham circumcised him just as God had commanded him to do with every male child born in his house. Abraham was a hundred years old and Sarah was ninety when Isaac was born.

One day when Isaac was a young boy, Sarah saw his older brother Ishmael making fun of Isaac. Sarah was not happy about what Ishmael was doing. Sarah told Abraham that Ishmael and his mother Hagar could no longer live with them, he should send them away. Abraham was not pleased with what Sarah said to him. Abraham prayed, and God told Abraham Sarah is right. Even though it was hard for him to do, Abraham had to tell Hagar she had to take her son and leave. Abraham gave them food and water and then sent them away. Hagar took her son, and they went to Egypt to live.

Years later, when Issac was a young man, God wanted to know how much Abraham loved him. He told Abraham to take Isaac, the son whom you love very much and offered him to Me as a burnt offering. Early the next morning Abraham loaded his donkey with the wood he needed to prepare the burnt offering; he took two of his servants and Isaac with him to go to Mount Moriah to offer his sacrifice. While on their way, Isaac said to Abraham, "Father, I see the wood and fire for the sacrifice but where is the burnt offering?" Abraham replied that God will provide. As they got to the mountain Abraham took the wood off the donkey and gave it to Isaac. He told his servants to wait for them while he and Isaac went to the top of the mountain to offer sacrifice to God.

They got to the top of the mountain and built the altar for the burnt offering. Abraham put Isaac on the altar to lie down and tied his hands and feet. As he raised the knife to offer Isaac, the angel of God called to him from heaven and said; "Abraham, Abraham do not hurt your son Isaac". Abraham looked in the direction of where he heard the voice, he saw the ram that God provided for him to offer as a burnt offering. The angel of the Lord called to Abraham from heaven a second time and said, *"I swear by myself, declares the Lord, that because you have done this and have not withheld your son, your only son, I will surely bless you and make your descendants as numerous as the stars in the sky and as the sand on the seashore. Your descendants will take possession of the cities of their enemies, and through your offspring all nations on earth will be blessed, because you have obeyed me."*
Genesis 22:16-18 NIV

LEARNING POINTS:

- God wants you to live to please Him
- God always does what He promises
- When your actions and words please God you will receive His blessings (rewards)
- God has a plan for your life
- Your faith in Yeshua (Jesus) gives you the courage to live and please God
- God does not expect you to be perfect, only obedient
- You can ask the Holy Spirit (Ruach HaKodesh) for help when you don't know the right thing to do

LESSON SUMMARY:

This lesson focuses on the birth of Isaac and his near sacrifice. It is a picture of Abraham's love and obedience to God. We can describe Abraham's life as **"Pleasing to God"** because he lived to please God. Abraham did what was pleasing to God. He didn't know where God wanted him to go when God told him to leave his family, but he obeyed and left. He obeyed God and circumcised all the men in his house, even Ismael, his son who was thirteen years old. Abraham was kind and generous, even to strangers. He believed that God would one day cause Sarah to have a son, as He promised.

After Abraham was circumcised, one day he was sitting by his tent door. The Lord Appeared to him. God promised Abraham that Sarah, his wife, would have a son even though they were both very old. Exactly one year later Sarah gave birth to a son and called his name Isaac. Life got a little hard for Abraham's family. Ishmael was making fun of Isaac, and Sarah was not pleased. She told Abraham, Ishmael and his mother "Hagar can no longer live with us. You must send them away". Sarah's words made Abraham sad. God spoke to Abraham and said, your wife Sarah is right, you must let Hagar and Ishmael go. Abraham gave them bread and water and then sent them away.

When Issac was a young man, God wanted to know if Abraham would still obey Him. He told Abraham to take Isaac and offer him as a sacrifice. God did not want Abraham to kill his son. Abraham took Isaac to the top of the mountain, built an altar, and put Isaac to lie down. He tied Isaac's hands and feet. Just as Abraham raised his hands with the knife to sacrifice Isaac, the angel of God called from heaven saying; Abraham, Abraham do not touch the boy. Abraham looked up and saw a ram in the bush next to him. God provided a ram for his sacrifice. Abraham offered the ram to God, then he and Isaac went home.

THE PROMISE CHILD: ISAAC

Genesis 18:1-4 NASB

Now the Lord appeared to him by the oaks of Mamre, while he was sitting at the tent door in the heat of the day. **2** *When he lifted up his eyes and looked, behold, three men were standing opposite him; and when he saw them, he ran from the tent door to meet them and bowed himself to the earth,* **3** *and said, "My Lord, if now I have found favor in Your sight, please do not pass Your servant by.* **4** *Please let a little water be brought and wash your feet, and rest yourselves under the tree;* **5** *and I will bring a piece of bread, that you may refresh yourselves; after that you may go on, since you have visited your servant." And they said, "So do, as you have said."*

Abraham asked Sarah to bake cakes for them, and then he went to his servant who took care of his flock and asked him to prepare one of the young calves for them to eat as well. When the food was ready Abraham took the cakes, the meat, and some milk to the men under the tree and they ate. One of the men, an angel, said to Abraham where is Sarah your wife? Abraham replied she is in the tent behind you. He said to Abraham; next year this time Sarah will have a child. Sarah laughed. Sarah laughed because she didn't see how it was possible for her to give birth to a child since both she and Abraham were very old. The angel reminded them that there is nothing too hard for God to do.

Scripture Reference Genesis 18:10-15 NASB

The angel said to Abraham, "I will surely return to you at this time next year; and behold, Sarah your wife will have a son." And Sarah was listening at the tent door, which was behind him. Now Abraham and Sarah were old, Sarah was past the age to have children. Sarah laughed to herself, saying, "After I have become old, shall I have pleasure, my lord being old also?" And the Lord said to Abraham, "Why did Sarah laugh, saying, 'Shall I indeed bear a child, when I am so old?' Is anything too difficult for the Lord? At the appointed time I will return to you, at this time next year, and Sarah will have a son." Sarah denied it however, saying, "I did not laugh"; for she was afraid. And He said, "No, but you did laugh."

THE BIRTH OF ISAAC, GENESIS 21

Now it was time for Sarah to give birth just as the angel told Abraham. It was fourteen years after God first told Abraham that his wife Sarah would give birth to a child before Issac was born. God promised Abraham that he would be the father of multitudes. All his children's children would be as many as the stars of the sky and as the sand of the sea, but there was one big problem; Sarah could not have children. Abraham and Sarah at first thought that God had somehow forgotten about His promise. Sarah, not wanting Abraham to live his life without a son, gave her servant Hagar to be his wife, hoping she will have a child for Abraham. Hagar we learned had a son whose name is Ishmael. Abraham thought Ishmael would be the one to inherit the promise God gave him. God told him no! Sarah will be the one to have a son to inherit My promise.

Scripture Reference Genesis 21:1-8 NASB
God remembered Sarah, **1** "and the Lord did for Sarah as He had promised. **2** So Sarah conceived and bore a son to Abraham in his old age, at the appointed time of which God had spoken to him. **3** Abraham called the name of his son who was born to him, whom Sarah bore to him, Isaac. **4** Then Abraham circumcised his son Isaac when he was eight days old, as God had commanded him. **5** Now Abraham was one hundred years old when his son Isaac was born to him. **6** Sarah said, "God has made laughter for me; everyone who hears will laugh with me." **7** And she said, "Who would have said to Abraham that Sarah would nurse children? Yet I have borne him a son in his old age." **8** The child grew and was weaned, and Abraham made a great feast on the day that Isaac was weaned.

LESSON DISCUSSION:

DO YOU LOVE ME?: A SACRIFICE OF OBEDIENCE

Can you imagine your parents telling you to give your favorite toy away? How would that make you feel?

That might have been the same way Abraham felt when God told him to bring Isaac (his only heir to the promise) and offer him as a sacrifice to Him (God). Abraham still obeyed God. God wanted to see how much Abraham loved Him.

Genesis 22:2 TLV
God said to him; *"Take your son, your only son whom you love—Isaac—and go to the land of Moriah, and offer him there as a burnt offering on one of the mountains about which I will tell you."*

Early the next morning Abraham loaded his donkey with the wood he needed to prepare the burnt offering; he took two of his servants and Isaac with him to go to Mount Moriah to offer his sacrifice. While on their way, Isaac said to Abraham, Father, I see the wood and fire for the sacrifice but where is the burnt offering?" Abraham replied God will provide. As they got to the mountain Abraham took the wood off the donkey and gave it to Isaac. He told his servants to wait for them while he and Isaac went to the top of the mountain to offer sacrifice to God.

They got to the top of the mountain and built the altar for the burnt offering. Abraham put Isaac on the altar to lie upon it and tied his hands and feet. As he raised the knife to offer Isaac, the angel of God called to him from heaven and said; Abraham, Abraham do not hurt your son Isaac. Abraham looked in the direction of where he heard the voice, it was then he saw the ram that God provided for him to offer as a burnt offering.

Genesis 22:16-18 NIV
The angel of the Lord called to Abraham from heaven a second time and said, *"I swear by myself, declares the Lord, that because you have done this and have not withheld your son, your only son, I will surely bless you and make your descendants as numerous as the stars in the sky and as the*

sand on the seashore. Your descendants will take possession of the cities of their enemies, and through your offspring all nations on earth will be blessed, because you have obeyed me."

YOUR WALK WITH GOD: LIVE TO PLEASE HIM!

Abraham and Sarah lived their lives to please God. They were not perfect but they were obedient. God blessed them because they were obedient and trusted His word.

When your actions and your words please God you will receive His rewards (blessings).

God's desire is for you and me to live a life pleasing to Him. Our faith in Yeshua (Jesus) gives us the courage to live and please God.

John 14:15-16
"If you love me, obey my commandments. 16 And I will ask the Father, and he will give you another Advocate, who will never leave you.

Colossians 2:6-7 NLT
And now, just as you accepted Christ Jesus as your Lord, you must continue to follow him. **7** Let your roots grow down into him, and let your lives be built on him. Then your faith will grow strong in the truth you were taught, and you will overflow with thankfulness.

You can ask the Holy Spirit (Ruach HaKodesh) to help you when you don't know the right thing to do.

Luke 24:49 NLT
"And now I will send the Holy Spirit, just as my Father promised. But stay here in the city until the Holy Spirit comes and fills you with power from heaven."

Romans 5:5b NLT
For we know how dearly God loves us, because he has given us the Holy Spirit to fill our hearts with his love.

Acts 11:12 NLT
The Holy Spirit told me (Peter) to go with them and not to worry that they were Gentiles.

What are some ways you can please God?

TURNING POINT:

A DIVIDED HOME, BUT GOD STILL HAS A PLAN.
GENESIS 21:9-20

One day when Isaac was a young boy, Sarah saw his older brother Ishmael making fun of Isaac. Sarah was not happy about what Ishmael was doing. Sarah told Abraham that Ishmael and his mother Hagar could no longer live with them, he should send them away. Abraham was not pleased with what Sarah said to him. Abraham prayed, and God told Abraham Sarah is right. Even though it was hard for him to do, Abraham had to tell Hagar she had to take her son and leave. Abraham gave them food and water and then sent them away. Hagar took her son, and they went to Egypt to live. Hagar and Ishmael were wandering in the desert for a while before their food and water ran out. Hagar did not know what to do when the water and food ran out so she left Ishmael under one of the bushes, then she went to the other side and cried. God heard her and the boy crying. An angel of God asked her what is the matter with you?

Ishmael was not the son God chose to inherit the promise He had to make Abraham's descendants as many as the stars of the sky or the sand of the sea, but God still had a plan for Ishmael. God promised to make Ishmael a great nation, just like Isaac.

Genesis 21: 17-21 TLV Then God heard the boy's voice and the angel of God called to Hagar from heaven, and He said to her, "What troubles you, Hagar? Do not be afraid, because God has heard the boy's voice where he is. **18** Get up! Lift the boy up, and hold on to him with your hand, for I will make him a great nation." **19** Then God opened her eyes and she saw a well of water, and she went and filled the water skin, and gave the boy a drink. **20** God was with the boy and he grew. He dwelled in the wilderness and became an archer. **21** He dwelled in the wilderness of Paran, and his mother took a wife for him from the land of Egypt.

God has a plan for your life, the same way He had a plan for Isaac and Ishmael. Pray and ask God, your heavenly Father to reveal His plan for your life.

PRACTICAL APPLICATIONS

FOR CHILDREN 4-6 YEARS OLD
- Tell them to think of their favorite toy, and then ask; if God told you to give it away would you be willing to do it?

- Pray and ask the Holy Spirit to give you a kind heart.

FOR CHILDREN 7-12 YEARS OLD
- Share your lunch at school with someone who is not your friend.

- Write down how sharing your lunch made you feel.

FOLLOW-UP FROM THE LAST TORAH PORTION
Ask who wants to share from last week's practical application

FOR CHILDREN 4-6 YEARS OLD
- Learn the first commandment with your parents. Exodus 20: 2

- Ask your parents to pray with you every night to hear God's voice.

FOR CHILDREN 7-12 YEARS OLD
- Learn the 1st and 5th Commandments. Exodus 20: 2 & 12

- Ask a close friend to let you know when you are not obedient to your teachers at school or other adults that give you right and Godly instructions.

- Ask the Holy Spirit to help you to hear God's voice and to be obedient even when it is hard.

QUESTIONS - TEACHERS ANSWER KEY

1. Where was Abraham sitting when he saw the three men?
At his tent's door

2. What is the name of Abraham's first son?
Ishmael

3. What did Sarah do when the men said she was going to have a son?
She laughed

4. How old was Isaac when he was circumcised?
Eight days old

5. Why did Sarah say Ishmael and his mother needed to leave?
Ishmael was making fun of Isaac

6. Where did Hagar and Ishmael go to live?
Egypt

7. What did God ask Abraham to do with Isaac?
Offer him as a sacrifice

8. What is the name of the Mountain Abraham went to sacrifice Isaac?
Moriah

9. Did God really want Abraham to kill his son?
No

10. What kind of animal did God provide for the sacrifice?
A Ram

11. Why was God pleased with Abraham?
He obeyed God's instructions

QUESTIONS - CHILDREN'S COPY

1. Where was Abraham sitting when he saw the three men?

2. What is the name of Abraham's first son?

3. What did Sarah do when the men said she was going to have a son?

4. How old was Isaac when he was circumcised?

5. Why did Sarah say Ishmael and his mother needed to leave?

6. Where did Hagar and Ishmael go to live?

7. What did God ask Abraham to do with Isaac?

8. What is the name of the Mountain Abraham went to sacrifice Isaac?

9. Did God really want Abraham to kill his son?

10. What kind of animal did God provide for the sacrifice?

11. Why was God pleased with Abraham?

CRAFTS FOR TORAH PORTION VAYERA

SUPPLIES:
White cardstock
Green construction paper
Red or Pink construction paper
Gems/studs
Cotton Balls
Doll eyes
Glue/glue stick
Markers/Crayons/Pencils

CRAFTS

1. Isaac's Birth Announcement Card!

Pre-draw Abraham/Sarah/Isaac. Make copies on cardstock, and cut them out. Pre-cut paper in the shape that could create a tent.

Pre-fold it to create creases, so the children could see how it should be folded. Glue a drawing in the middle as shown. Color it!

Fold it to look like a tent. Glue on both sides. Then glue the paper tent to a card stock at the top of the page. Glue pre-cut strips of green cardstock so it looks like grass. Draw grass on it.

Decorate the tent with gems and studs! Mark the card with "Welcome Baby Isaac!", "From Abraham and Sarah!" Be creative!

THE FINISH WORK

2. "Behold a Ram!" Activity.

Give out pre-drawn cardstock with the ram. Have the children color the horns and legs. Then take cotton balls and glue them as shown! Glue doll eyes (not shown on the drawing, as still waiting for it in the mail). Trace "Behold a Ram"

Chayei Sarah
"The Life of Sarah"

Torah Portion 5:

Chayei Sarah - The Life of Sarah

Scriptures:

Genesis 23:1–25:18, 1 Kings 1:1–31, John 4:3-14, Psalm 45

Chayei Sarah is Hebrew for ***"Life of Sarah"*** or ***"Sarah's Life"***; it is found in the first verse of our Torah Portion.

Genesis 23:1 TLV

Now Sarah's life was 127 years—the years of Sarah's life.

The Theme of the Torah Portion:

The Goodness of God and Helping Others

Genesis 24:27

"Blessed be *Adonai*, the God of my master Abraham, who has not forsaken His loyalty and His truth toward my master. As for me, *Adonai* has guided me in the way to the house of my master's brothers."

Torah Portion Outline

Genesis Chapter 23:1-2
- Sarah Dies at 127 Years Old
- Abraham Purchased a Field to Bury Her, **Genesis 23: 3-20**

Genesis 24
- Abraham Sends His Servant to Find a Wife for Isaac **Genesis 24:1-15**
- The Servant Meets Rebekah, **Genesis 24:15-27**
- Meeting Rebekah's Parents and Brother Laban, **Genesis 24:28-57**
- Rebekah Agrees to go with Abraham's Servant, **Genesis 24:58-61**
- Isaac Marries Rebekah, **Genesis 24:62-67**

Genesis Chapter 25
- Abraham Married Keturah, **Genesis 25: 1-6**
- He Died at 137 Years of Age. He is Buried by Ishmael and Isaac, **Genesis 25: 7-11**
- Ishmael's Descendants, **Genesis 25:12-18**

LESSON SUMMARY:

This Torah Portion begins with the words "Now Sarah lived…" The "Life of Sarah" describes how Abraham mourns for Sarah after she dies at 127 years old. Abraham purchased a field from one of the families among the people where he lived as a stranger so he could bury Sarah in the cave. This cave became very famous. It is known as the Cave of Machpelah.

Abraham was very old and he too would one day die, but he did not want to leave Isaac alone. He asked one of his servants, who worked for him for a very long time, to help him find a wife for Isaac. The servant was willing to help but Abraham had one special request. "He said to the servant, do not look for a wife among the women of the country where we live but go far away to the country where I was born. The servant asked, what if I go and find the girl to be Isaac's wife and she doesn't want to come back with me? What should I do? Abraham told him the God of heaven and earth will go before you and prepare her heart, but even then if she still does not want to come, do not take my son to my country." The servant agreed and said okay.

Early the next morning the servant took ten camels with gifts of gold, silver, and beautiful garments and left to find Isaac a wife. He also brought a few of the other servants with him. When the servant got to the country where Abraham was born he stopped at a well to get water for him and the camels to drink. Before he got the water, he prayed to God. He said, "God of my master Abraham, show kindness to me just as you showed kindness to my master and help me find a wife for my master's son. May it be when I see her and I ask her for a drink of water, if she gives me water to drink and says she will also give my camels water then I will know she is the right one."

Just before he finished praying, the servant saw Rebekah coming to the well. He said to her; "please give me some water to drink. She took her jug of water and gave him water to drink." She also gave his camels water to drink just as he prayed. The servant was happy that God answered his prayer. He asked Rebekah who her father was. She told him who she was and where she lived. The servant was even more excited that she was exactly the person Abraham was hoping he would find. He bowed down to the ground and worshiped God for helping him find the right person to be Isaac's wife. He told Rebekah that he worked for Abraham, her father's brother. He gave her gold bracelets, earrings, and a nose ring as gifts. Rebekah was very happy and excited, she left her water jars and ran to tell her family all about the servant.

When she got home and told her parents and brother Laban about the servant, she showed them the gifts that he gave her. They asked where he was, and why didn't you bring him home with you. Her brother, Laban ran to the well to meet the servant. Laban told the servant to come and stay with him and his family. They prepared a place for him and the men with him and also his camels. The servant was happy to go with Laban.

When they got to the house, Laban and his family prepared a meal for the servant and all the men with him, but the servant refused to eat before he told them why he was there. So they listened to all that he told them and how Abraham made him promise to find a wife for Isaac in his country but not to bring Isaac. He told of all the wealth and blessings Abraham received from God. He also told them of his prayer and as soon as he was about to finish praying Rebekah showed up. He said that is how he knew he was in the right place. They all agreed that it was God who sent him. Then they all ate.

The next morning the servant said to Rebekah's family he was going to leave and wanted to take Rebekah with him. Laban, her brother, and mother said to him stay to with us for ten more days then we will send her with you. The servant knowing God gave him favor answered, "I don't want to wait since God has made it possible for me to find you. Please let me go and Rebekah also. They responded we will ask her if she is willing to go with you." So they called Rebekah and asked her if she wanted to go with the servant, and she said yes. So they sent Rebekah with him and her nurse.

The evening they arrived home, Isaac was in the field praying; he looked up and in the distance, he saw camels coming. As they got closer to their home, Rebekah looked up and she saw a man in the field. She asked the servant, "who is that man in the field coming towards us? The servant replied that is my master." She put her veil over her face and got down from the camel.

When Rebekah met Isaac, the servant told Isaac the story of the trip. Isaac took Rebekah to his mother's tent. He married her and she became his wife.

LESSON DISCUSSION:

BEING A HELPER AND ASKING GOD FOR HELP

Teaching Points:

In the story, we learned some very important lessons:
1. God was good to Abraham. He blessed Abraham and gave his servant favor with Rebekah's family.

2. Abraham loved Isaac. He only wanted the best wife for him.

3. Abraham trusted his servant. He knew his servant would obey his request to find a wife for Isaac.

4. The servant and Rebekah were helpful. The servant was willing to travel many miles to Abraham's home country to find a wife for Isaac. Rebekah was willing to help the servant. She gave him, and all the men, and his camels water to drink.

5. God answers prayers. He answered Abraham's prayer. He also answered the servant's prayer.

BEING A HELPER AND ASKING GOD FOR HELP

God is always our helper. He promises to be our help even when we are in trouble. Just as the servant prayed and asked God for help to find a wife for Isaac, you too can pray and ask Him for help.

Psalm 54:4 NLT But God is my helper. The Lord keeps me alive!

What are some of the things you can ask God for help with?

It is very important for us to be helpful to those who need our help, especially to those who are not able to help themselves.

Can you think of ways you can be helpful to:
1. Parents
2. Teachers
3. Friends
4. Someone at school who is not your friend

Last week we learned in Torah Portion Vayera "He Appeared," how God tested Abraham to see how much he loved Him. He asked Abraham to offer Isaac as a sacrifice. He did not want Abraham to kill his son. He only wanted to know if he would obey. Abraham was obedient and took Isaac to the top of the mountain, and just as he raised the knife an angel from heaven called his name two times. When Abraham looked to see where the voice came from he saw a ram caught in the bush. God provided a ram to take Isaac's place as the sacrifice.

Do you know who else God gave to become a sacrifice? (Allow feedback from children before giving them the answer)

God gave Yeshua to be a sacrifice for us so that we can have a relationship with Him. He loves us so much that He gave us the Holy Spirit to be our helper when Yeshua went back to be with Him in heaven.

John 3:16 NLT "For this is how God loved the world: He gave his one and only Son, so that everyone who believes in him will not perish but have eternal life.

You are never alone! You can always pray and ask God for help.

TURNING POINT:

WHEN TRAGEDY STRIKES

Have you ever lost someone you love? Maybe a family member, a friend, or even a pet. How did you feel?

Even if you have never lost someone you love or a pet, close your eyes for a moment and try to think about how Abraham must have felt when Sarah, his wife whom he loved very much, died.

Abraham and Sarah spent many years of their lives together. I can imagine that Sarah was his best friend. Now he was alone without his best friend and the mother of his son. His beautiful wife, Sarah!

Abraham wanted to honor Sarah's life and her memories so he purchased a field to bury her.

Genesis 23:7-9 NASB

So Abraham rose and bowed to the people of the land, the sons of Heth. **8** And he spoke with them, saying, "If it is your wish *for me* to bury my dead out of my sight, hear me, and approach Ephron the son of Zohar for me, **9** that he may give me the cave of Machpelah which he owns, which is at the end of his field; for the full price let him give it to me in your presence for a burial site."

When we lose a loved one it can be a very difficult time, but we do not have to go through it alone. We have the Holy Spirit, who is our Comforter. He will comfort us in our pain and give us peace. God also will send family and friends to help us when we are hurting.

We can follow Abraham's example and do something that will honor the person's life and memory to help us in those difficult times.

If you are experiencing a difficult time. I pray that God, our Heavenly Father will send the Holy Spirit to comfort you and give you peace. I pray that He will also send someone to talk with you.

PRACTICAL APPLICATIONS

FOR CHILDREN 4-6 YEARS OLD
Be your mommy's helper this week.

FOR CHILDREN 7-12 YEARS OLD
Be helpful to your parents this week. Help a friend who is having a hard
time fitting in at school.

FOLLOW-UP FROM THE LAST TORAH PORTION
Ask who wants to share from last week's practical application.

FOR CHILDREN 4-6 YEARS OLD
- Tell them to think of their favorite toy, and then ask; if God told you to give it away would you be willing to do it?

- Pray and ask the Holy Spirit to give you a kind heart.

FOR CHILDREN 7-12 YEARS OLD
- Share your lunch at school with someone who is not your friend.

- Write down how sharing your lunch made you feel.

QUESTIONS - TEACHERS ANSWER KEY

1. **How old was Sarah when she died?**
   127 years old

2. **What was the name of the field Abraham bought?**
   Machpelah

3. **Who did Abraham send to find Isaac a wife?**
   His oldest servant

4. **How many camels did the servant take with him?**
   10

5. **Where did the servant meet Rebekah?**
   At the well

6. **What did the servant ask Rebekah for?**
   Water to drink

7. **Name one of the gifts the servant gave Rebekah.**
   Gold bracelet, earrings, or nose ring

8. **What is the name of Rebekah's brother?**
   Laban

9. **What is the name of Isaac's wife?**
   Rebekah

10. **What was Isaac doing when he saw the camels coming with Rebekah?**
    Praying

QUESTIONS - CHILDREN'S COPY

1. How old was Sarah when she died?

2. What was the name of the field Abraham bought?

3. Who did Abraham send to find Isaac a wife?

4. How many camels did the servant take with him?

5. Where did the servant meet Rebekah?

6. What did the servant as Rebekah for?

7. Name one of the gifts the servant gave Rebekah.

8. What is the name of Rebekah's brother?

9. What is the name of Isaac's wife?

10. What was Isaac doing when he saw the camels coming with Rebekah?

CRAFTS FOR TORAH PORTION CHAYEI SARAH

SUPPLIES:
Beige or brown color cardstock
White cardstock
Popsicle sticks
Gems/stickers/sequins
Paper fasteners
Glue
Stickers of birds
Markers/pencils

CRAFTS "THE CAMEL AND THE WELL"

a) Glue popsicle sticks on beige color cardstock in the form of a well! About 10 sticks vertically together, then 2 across, then 4 up, and another across. Follow exactly as shown.

b) While the sticks are drying, color the pre-cut camel's head and body. Then decorate the saddle of the camel. The children need to be creative and use gems, stickers, and sequins to decorate in the way that they want.

c) Then take paper fasteners and connect the head and neck of the camel to the body. <u>Please note that the holes are already poked for the children</u>!

How fun with the head of the camel as they move up and down!

Glue the body of the camel on the paper as shown. <u>Only the bodies, not necks/heads.</u>

d) Draw the sun and put bird stickers.
e) If additional time allows, the children could color the well.

THE FINISHED WORK

Toldot
"History"

Torah Portion 6:
Toldot "Generations or History"

Scriptures:
Genesis 25:19-28:9, Malachi 1:2-7, Psalm 36, Matthew 10:21-38

Toldot is the Hebrew word translated as **"Generations"** or **"History"**. It is found in the first verse of our Torah Portion.

Genesis 25:19
Now these are ***the records of the generations*** of Isaac, Abraham's son: Abraham became the father of Isaac.

The Theme of the Torah Portion:

Unusual Things

Genesis 25: 22 -26 The children struggled together within her. She said, "If it is like this, why do I live?" She went to inquire of Yahweh. **23** Yahweh said to her, "Two nations are in your womb. Two peoples will be separated from your body. The one people will be stronger than the other people. The elder will serve the younger." **24** When her days to be delivered were fulfilled, behold, there were twins in her womb. **25** The first came out red all over, like a hairy garment. They named him Esau. **26** After that, his brother came out, and his hand had hold on Esau's heel. He was named Jacob. Isaac was sixty years old when she bore them.

Torah Portion Outline

Genesis 25:1-34
- Rebekah's Barrenness and Pregnancy, **Gen.25:19-23**
- The Birth of Esau and Jacob, **Gen.25:24-28**
- Esau Sells his Birthright, **Gen.25:29-34**

Genesis 26:1-34
- Isaac Lives in Gerar Because of Famine, **Gen.26:1-11**
- God Blesses Isaac, **Gen.26:12-25**
- Isaac and Abimelech Make a Covenant, **Gen.26:26-34**

Genesis 27:1-47
- Isaac's Decision to Bless Esau, **Gen.27:1-4**
- Rebekah's Scheme to Deceive Isaac, **Gen.27:5-17**
- Jacob Deceives Isaac and Receives Esau's Blessing, **Gen. 27:18-30**
- Esau Returns for His Blessing, **Gen.27:31-40**
- Esau's Hatred Towards Jacob, **Gen.27:41**
- Jacob is Sent to Laban, **Gen.27:42-47**

Genesis 28:1-9
Isaac Warns Jacob Not to Marry a Canaanite Woman, **Gen.28:1-5**
Esau Marries the Daughter of Ishmael, **Gen.28:6-9**

LESSON SUMMARY:

Do you know your family history? Do you know the name of your cousins and uncles? In this week's Torah Portion, we learn about the life of Isaac and Rebekah after they got married. We also learn about the family history of Abraham's eldest son Ishmael. Ishmael had twelve sons, who were also princes of their tribes. Ishmael lived until he was 137 years old. Mostly we learn about the life of Isaac and Rebekah as they grow together as a family.

Rebekah could not have children just like Sarah. Isaac prayed to God for her and God answered his prayer. Twenty years after they were married Rebekah became pregnant. One day she wasn't feeling well, and she thought something was wrong with the baby inside her tummy. She went to pray and ask the Lord what was happening. The Lord told her she was having twins. The babies He told her represent two nations and they were fighting with each other. God also told her, one will be stronger than the other, and the older will serve the younger.

When it was time for her to give birth, she had the twins as the Lord told her. The firstborn was Esau. He was red and had hair all over his body. The second was Jacob. He was born holding on to Esau's heel. As the boys grew older it was obvious they did not enjoy doing the same things. Esau loved being outside and hunting with his father, but Jacob loved staying at home with his mother. Esau was very proud because he was loved by his father and he knew as the firstborn he would inherit everything his father had.

One day Esau came home from the field where he was hunting. He was tired and hungry. Jacob was cooking some lentil stew. Esau asked Jacob for some of his stew. Jacob said to him, "you have to give me the rights of the firstborn before I give you my stew." Esau was hungry and didn't think about what Jacob was saying. "He said to Jacob, you can have my birthright. What good can it do for me now that I am hungry and about to die?" Jacob said to him, "not until you swear to me, that I can have it." Esau swore to give Jacob his birthright, then Jacob gave him bread and lentil stew to eat.

Years later, when Jacob was old and could hardly see, he called Esau his firstborn. Esau responded, "Here I am. Jacob said to him; I can hardly see and I don't know when I am going to die. Take your bow and your weapons and go hunt some venison for me, then make some of my favorite food that I may eat and bless you before I die." Esau went to the field to hunt for his dad.

Rebekah heard when Isaac spoke to Esau. Rebekah said to Jacob; *"Go now to the flock and get me two good young goats from there. I will make them savory food for your father, such as he loves. You shall bring it to your father, that he may eat, so that he may bless you before his death."*
Genesis 25:9-10

Jacob answered his mother, Rebekah; *"Esau my brother is a hairy man, and I am a smooth man. What if my father touches me? I will seem to him as a deceiver, and I would bring a curse on myself, and not a blessing."* His mother said to him, *"Let your curse be on me, my son. Only obey my voice, and go get them for me."* **Genesis 25:11-13.**

Jacob obeyed his mother and did just as she told him. She prepared the goat for Jacob the way he loved his food. She also put some of the goat's hair on Jacob's hands and neck, just in case Isaac decided to touch him. Jacob put on Esau's favorite clothes then brought the food to Isaac and pretended to be Esau. Isaac was hesitant to eat because Esau returned earlier than unusual from the field. He also noticed that the person who brought him the food sounded like Jacob and not Esau. Jacob wasn't sure who it was that brought him the food because he could hardly see, so he told his son, "come near to me so I can touch your hands and smell your clothes." He still wasn't convinced that it was Esau, but he ate the food and then gave his blessing.

A few minutes after Isaac blessed Jacob and he left, Esau came in with the food he prepared. Isaac was a little confused and said, "who are you?" "Esau answered I am your son, your firstborn." Then Isaac realized it was Jacob who came in and deceived him and got the blessing of the firstborn. Esau became angry that he did not get the blessing. He cried and asked, "do you only have one blessing father, can't you bless me too?" Esau made a vow to kill his brother once his father dies. Rebekah heard of Esau's vow and told Isaac to send Jacob away to her brother Laban, for him to find a wife. When Esau learned that his parents sent Jacob away to find a wife because they did not want him to marry any of the women in the country they lived in, Esau went and got married to one of the women just to make his parents mad.

LESSON DISCUSSION:

WHEN UNUSUAL THINGS HAPPEN

In this Torah Portion, we see some unusual things happen between Jacob and his brother Esau even before they were born.

1. They were fighting in their mother's tummy
2. Jacob was born holding Esau's heel
3. Esau sold his birthright for a pot of lentil stew
4. Rebekah and Issac trick Jacob to get the firstborn blessing
5. Esau marries women who don't please his parents
6. Esau threatened to kill Jacob

Unusual things can be good or bad:
Though it was unusual for Esau to sell his birthright for stew, and for Jacob to trick his father Isaac for the blessing of the firstborn, which are both bad examples of how siblings should treat each other. It is also good because we learn that Esau was not a responsible person to inherit the blessing God promised, Isaac and Abraham.

Ask what was the blessing, to see if they remember. *(They might give you their version)*

I will bless you and make your name great. Your descendants will be like the sand of the sea and the stars of the sky.

Yeshua did many good unusual things.
He healed the sick. Raised the dead. Walked on water. Turned water into wine. He loved people whom others did not love.

Can you think of other unusual things Yeshua did while he was on Earth?

What are some unusual things that are happening around us today?
Allow children to give their answers before you give your examples.

How should we respond to people who do unusual things?
When people do bad and unusual things we can either become angry like Esau and try to get revenge, or we can be like Yeshua and ask our heavenly Father to help us to love and forgive them.

When people do good unusual things, we should ask the Holy Spirit if the good they are doing is from God, or if they are trying to trick us like Jacob tricked his father Isaac.

When it is from God we can thank Him for the good that they are doing and allow God to teach us how to help.

Do you want to do unusual things for God?
Pray with children and ask God to give them boldness like Joshua, David, Daniel, Deborah, Esther, and Mary.

TURNING POINT:

HISTORY REPEATS ITSELF

King Solomon, the wisest man who ever lived once said, *there is nothing new under the sun, What has been is what will be, and what has been done is what will be done. Ecclesiastes 1:9*

In this Torah Portion, we see a picture of what King Solomon meant. In the Torah Portion Vayera, Abraham went to live in Egypt because there was a famine in the land of Canaan where he lived, (Genesis 12:10). Abraham also went to Gerar and lived, (Genesis 20). Do you remember what he asked Sarah to do? He asked her to tell everyone that she was his sister so they would not kill him and take her away. He was afraid, so he asked her to lie. Was it right for him to lie? No, but God protected Sarah, even though Abimelech took her from Abraham and brought her to his house.

We also learn that Isaac also had to leave Canaan because there was a famine in the land. God told him not to go to Egypt. Isaac went to live in Philistia, in Gerar. Gerar is the same place where Abraham lived. **Genesis 26:1-2** *Now there was a famine in the land, besides the previous famine that had occurred in the days of Abraham. So Isaac went to Gerar, to Abimelech king of the Philistines. The Lord appeared to him and said, "Do not go down to Egypt; stay in the land of which I shall tell you.*

Like his father, Isaac too, was afraid to let everyone know that Rebekah was his wife. He told her not to let anyone know that she was his wife, but his sister. Isaac did the same thing his father did. He lied to save his life. God was not pleased with his lie, but He protected Rebekah.

Genesis 26:6-11 *So Isaac lived in Gerar.* **7** *When the men of the place asked about his wife, he said, "She is my sister," for he was afraid to say, "my wife," thinking, "the men of the place might kill me on account of Rebekah, for she is beautiful."* **8** *It came about, when he had been there a long time, that Abimelech king of the Philistines looked out through a window, and saw, and behold, Isaac was caressing his wife Rebekah.* **9** *Then Abimelech called Isaac and said, "Behold, certainly she is your wife!*

How then did you say, 'She is my sister'?" And Isaac said to him, "Because I said, 'I might die on account of her.'" **10** *Abimelech said, "What is this you have done to us? One of the people might easily have lain with your wife, and you would have brought guilt upon us."* **11** *So Abimelech charged all the people, saying, "He who touches this man or his wife shall surely be put to death."*

Have you ever been afraid to tell your parents, teachers, or an adult the truth because you did not want to get in trouble when you did something wrong?

How many times did they ask you a question hoping that you will tell the truth?

God showed Abraham and Isaac grace when they lied to Abimelech because He knew they were afraid to die. God would have protected them even if they had told the truth. In the same way when your parents and teachers ask you the same question more than once they are showing you grace waiting for you to tell the truth.

Next time when you do something wrong, don't be afraid to tell the truth. Speak the truth knowing that God is watching and listening. He will allow your parents and teachers to give you grace even if you receive punishment for your actions.

PRACTICAL APPLICATIONS

FOR CHILDREN 4-6 YEARS OLD
Ask your parents to read to you the story of Samuel.
1 Samuel chapter 2:18-20; chapter 3.

Listen for the voice of God every night for Him to call your name.

FOR CHILDREN 7-12 YEARS OLD
Read to you the story of Samuel. 1 Samuel 2:18-20; chapter 3.

Pray and ask God to show you one unusual thing He wants you to do this week. Write down what He tells you, then share it with your parents and ask them for help to do it.

FOLLOW-UP FROM THE LAST TORAH PORTION
Ask who wants to share from last week's practical application

FOR CHILDREN 4-6 YEARS OLD
Be your mommy's helper this week.

FOR CHILDREN 7-12 YEARS OLD
Be helpful to your parents this week. Help a friend who is having a hard
time fitting in at school.

QUESTIONS - TEACHERS ANSWER KEY

1. Who is Ishmael?
Abraham's oldest son or Isaac's brother

2. How old was Ishmael when he died?
137 years old

3. How many sons did Ishmael have?
12 sons

4. Why did Rebekah feel sick when she was pregnant?
The babies were fighting

5. Why did God say they were fighting?
There would represent two nations

6. Who was the oldest son?
Esau

7. What was unusual about the way they were born?
Jacob was holding onto Esau's heel

8. What did Jacob ask Esau for before he gave him the stew?
His birthright

9. What kind of animal did Rebekah prepare for Isaac to eat?
Goat

10. What did Rebekah use to cover Jacobs's hands?
Goat's hair

11. Where was Jacob sent to live?
With Rebekah's brother Laban (or to her country)

QUESTIONS - CHILDREN'S COPY

1. Who is Ishmael?

2. How old was Ishmael when he died?

3. How many sons did Ishmael have?

4. Why did Rebekah feel sick when she was pregnant?

5. Why did God say they were fighting?

6. Who was the oldest son?

7. What was unusual about the way they were born?

8. What did Jacob ask Esau for before he gave him the stew?

9. What kind of animal did Rebekah prepare for Isaac to eat?

10. What did Rebekah use to cover Jacobs's hands?

11. Where was Jacob sent to live?

CRAFT FOR TORAH PORTION TOLDOT

SUPPLIES:
Bright Color Cardstock
Colorful construction paper
Glue and glue sticks
Scissors
Lentils
Doll plastic eyes
Markers/pencils
Cotton balls

ACTIVITY: BIRTHRIGHT AND STEW

a) Children will receive pre-cut little people to represent Jacob and Esau. Glue Jacob on the left top side and Esau on the bottom right of the bright color cardstock.

b) Children will receive pre-cut components for Jacob and Esau. First allow the children to glue Jacob's components: black hair, blue shirt, and black shorts. Then allow the children to Esau components: red hair and beard and a red cover-up.

c) Then the children will draw the belt and shoes for Jacob, and glue the eyes on him. Proceed to draw the belt, shoes, and bow for Esau. Glue the eyes on him as well. Finish with gluing cotton balls on Esau's chest, hair, and legs. Color in red.

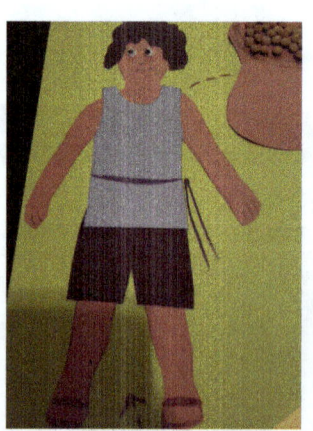 

d) Children will receive the bowl and birthright cutouts. Glue them as shown on the finished artwork.

e) Take lentils and glue them with glue on the bowl to represent the stew.

f) Mark Jacob and Esau. Then show with the arrows how the exchange happened with exchanging birthright for a stew.

COMPLETED ARTWORK

VAYETZE

"He went Out"

Torah Portion 7:

Vayetze - He Went Out

Scriptures:

Genesis 28:10-32:3, Hosea 11:7-12:14,
Psalm 3, John 1:41-51

Vayetze is the Hebrew word for the phrase *"went out"* in the first verse of our Torah Portion.

Genesis 28:10 WEB

Jacob *went out* from Beersheba, and went toward Haran.

The Theme of the Torah Portion:
A Work of Love

Genesis 29: 20
Jacob served seven years for Rachel. They seemed to him but a few days, for the love he had for her.

Torah Portion Outline

Genesis 28:10-22
- Jacob's Ladder From Heaven, **Gen.28:10-16**
- Jacob Builds an Altar to God, **Gen.28:17-22**

Genesis 29:1-35
- Jacob Meets and Loves Rachel, **Gen.29:1-13**
- Jacob's Work Agreement With Laban to Marry Rachel, **Gen.29:14-21**
- Laban Substitutes Leah for Rachel, **Gen.29:22-26**
- Jacob Works Seven More Years for Rachel, **Gen.29:27-30**
- Leah Bears Four Sons, **Gen.29:31-35**

Genesis 30: 1-43
- Rachel Gives Her Maid Billah to Jacob, **Gen.30:1-12**
- Rachel Bargains for Jacob, **Gen.30:13-16**
- Leah's Last Three Children, **Gen.30:17-21**
- Rachel Conceives and Gave Birth to Joseph, **Gen.30:18-26**
- Jacob's Contract Agreement With Laban Before He Leaves, **Gen.30:27-35**
- Laban's new deceit, **Gen.30:36-43**

Genesis 31:1-32:3
- Jacob Secretly Leaves Laban, **Gen.31:1-21**
- God Warns Laban in His Pursuit to Find Jacob, **Gen.31:22-24**
- Laban Confronts Jacob, **Gen.31:25-43**
- Laban Proposes a Treaty **Gen.31:44-32:3**

LESSON SUMMARY:

In last week's Torah Portion, we learned that Jacob deceived his father Isaac, and got the blessing that was for his older brother Esau. Esau was angry and vowed to kill him once their father died. Their mother, Rebekah, heard about Esau's vow and told Isaac to send Jacob to her brother Laban to protect him. Isaac called Jacob and blessed him and sent him to go to his uncle Laban, he also told Jacob not to marry any of the women from Canaan where they lived but to find a wife where his uncle lives.

In this week's Torah Portion, we learn about Jacob's journey and his life with his uncle Laban. Jacob went from his home in Beersheba and went toward Haran where his uncle Laban lived. On his journey, he came to a place and stayed there all night. That night he had a dream. In his dream, he saw a ladder and the top of it reached heaven. He also saw angels walking back and forth from heaven to earth. The Lord was standing above the ladder. He called Jacob and said; *"I am the Lord God of Abraham thy father, and the God of Isaac: the land whereon thou liest, to thee will I give it, and to thy seed; And thy seed shall be as the dust of the earth, and thou shalt spread abroad to the west, and to the east, and to the north, and to the south: and in thee and in thy seed shall all the families of the earth be blessed. And, behold, I am with thee, and will keep thee in all places whither thou goest, and will bring thee again into this land; for I will not leave thee, until I have done that which I have spoken to thee of."* **Genesis 28:13-15**

Upon hearing the voice of God Jacob was awakened from his sleep. He said, "this must be where God lives and I did not know." He was very afraid, for he thought this place must be the house of God and the gateway to heaven. Jacob got up early that morning and took the stones that he used as his pillows and built an altar and poured oil on it. He then named the place Bethel which means house of God. Jacob made a vow saying, *"If God will be with me, and will keep me in this way that I go, and will give me bread to eat, and clothes to put on, So that I come again to my father's house in peace; then will the Lord be my God: And this stone, which I have set for a pillar, will be God's house: and of all that thou shalt give me I will surely give the tenth to Him."* **Genesis 28:19-22**

Jacob continued his journey. He came to a field where he saw shepherds taking care of sheep by a well. He asked them if they knew Laban. They answered him yes, we know him. He inquired if he was well. They responded he is well. Then they said to him here comes his daughter Rachel. Rachel was a beautiful young girl. Jacob fell in love with her the moment he saw her. He was so fascinated by her beauty he rolled a huge stone from the well by himself and gave water to all the animals she brought to the field. Jacob was happy to meet Rachel. He told her that his mother was her father's sister Rebekah. Rachel was also excited to meet Jacob. She ran home and told her father Laban about him. Laban came out to the well to meet Jacob. Jacob told Laban everything that happened and why he came to visit him. Laban was pleased to know that Jacob was his nephew.

LESSON DISCUSSION:

AM I DREAMING?

Rebekah loved Jacob, she always remembered the message God gave her when she was pregnant. God told her she would give birth to twins. They will become two nations, one will be stronger than the other, and the older will serve the younger. When she heard Isaac telling Esau to go and hunt game and bring him his favorite food so he could eat and bless him before he did, she must have thought that Isaac did not know that it was Jacob who was to become the nation that will rule. Jacob along with his mother tricked Isaac and got the blessing of the firstborn that was intended for Esau. Esau was angry and wanted to kill him. Jacob had to leave home because his mother loved him and did not want Esau to kill him. Jacob's parents sent him to live with his uncle Laban. We are not told if Jacob knew where he was going.

How would you feel if you had to live with a family you have never met?

On his journey, he stopped at a place and spent the night. While he was there he had a dream. In his dream, he saw a ladder with angels walking up and down the ladder. He also heard the voice of God. Everything seemed real to Jacob. He thought he was in the place where God lives. He built an altar with the stones he used as his pillow while he slept. He named the place Bethel, even though the name was Luz.

Have you ever had a dream and woke up thinking it was real?

Can you imagine how Jacob felt when He heard God's voice calling him?

Jacob must have felt abandoned by his family. He was sent to go and live with a family he did not know. God revealed Himself to Jacob in a dream and reminded him that he is not alone. God said to him; *I am with you, and I will watch over you wherever you go, and I will bring you back to this*

land, for I will not forsake you until I have done what I promised you."
Genesis 28:15

Do you think this was the first time Jacob heard God's voice?

How do you think you would react if you heard God's voice calling your name?

Can you remember a time your parents told you to do something you didn't want to do?

Every parent loves their children and only wants the best for them. When your parents tell you to do something even if you don't understand why, just know it is never to hurt you.

When you are obedient to your parents and teachers. God is pleased with you. When Yeshua was on earth, he was obedient to his earthly parents and God, His heavenly Father. He said; "everything I do is what my Father in Heaven tells me."

God was pleased with him. When Yeshua was immersed in water, the Father sent the Holy Spirit in the form of a dove and it rested on him. Then God said, "this is My Son, I am pleased with him."

God is looking for those who will love Him with all their heart and live obediently to His commandments.

You can live a life pleasing to God our heavenly Father as believers in Yeshua. Today ask the Father to give you a heart of obedience and allow the Holy Spirit to teach you His ways.

TURNING POINT:

NOT MY CHOICE

Every time we are given a choice to choose what we want, we always choose what we think is the best. In this week's lesson we learn our choice is not always what we receive.

Our lesson continues from the last Torah Portion when Jacob left his home to go live with his uncle Laban.

When Jacob met his uncle Laban at first things seemed to be going well. Jacob agrees to work for Laban. Laban said to him, not because you are my relative should I make you work for free. What should I pay you? Laban had two daughters Rachel and Leah. Rachel was the younger and more beautiful of the two sisters. Jacob loved Rachel. He asked Laban to marry Rachel as payment for his work. Laban agreed to give Rachel to Jacob as his wife. Jacob had to work for Laban for seven years before he could marry her. Jacob had a great love for Rachel so the seven years he had to work were like just a few days to him.

For seven years Jacob served Laban and also prepared for when he would marry Rachel. When it was time for Jacob to marry Rachel, he went to Laban and said give me my wife, for I have completed all my years of work. Laban gathered all the people and held a great feast. In the evening Laban brought his older daughter Leah to Jacob. He brought her to his tent and she became his wife. Jacob did not know it was Leah until morning because he had too much wine to drink. In the morning when he was awake, he realized that Laban had tricked him and given Leah to be his wife instead of Rachel. Jacob went to Laban and said, "why did you trick me? I worked seven years for Rachel and you have given me Leah, she is not my choice." Laban answered, "it is not our custom to give the younger daughter in marriage before the older one. If you work for me for seven more years I will also give you Rachel to be your wife." Jacob agreed to serve Laban for seven more years because he loved Rachel.

Jacob had to leave home because he tricked his father Isaac and got Esau's blessing. Now he had been tricked by Laban.

In the last Torah Portion, we also learned about some unusual things that happened in Jacob's family. Today, we see where Laban tells him it is unusual for the younger daughter to be married before the older daughter. Jacob had to remain with Leah even though she was not his choice for a wife.

What can we learn from the lives of Jacob and Laban?
1. Sometimes we may not get what we want but God is still in control.
2. Not everything we want or desire is a part of God's plan for us.
3. Parents always want what's best for their children.

Next time you are given something you didn't choose, ask your heavenly Father to help you appreciate what you have received.

Have you ever thought something very unfair happened to you, but it turned out to be for the best?

PRACTICAL APPLICATIONS

FOR CHILDREN 4-6 YEARS OLD

Ask your parents to show you a picture of a family member you don't know. Ask if you can call and talk with him or her.

FOR CHILDREN 7-12 YEARS OLD

Make a list of three things you want. Ask your heavenly Father if these are His choice for you.

Listen for Him to answer during the week. Write each of His answers next to what you want.

Write about how His answer made you feel.

FOLLOW-UP FROM THE LAST TORAH PORTION

Ask who wants to share from last week's practical application

FOR CHILDREN 4-6 YEARS OLD

Ask your parents to read to you the story of Samuel.
1 Samuel chapter 2:18-20; chapter 3.

Listen for the voice of God every night for Him to call your name.

FOR CHILDREN 7-12 YEARS OLD

Read to you the story of Samuel. 1 Samuel 2:18-20; chapter 3.

Pray and ask God to show you one unusual thing He wants you to do this week. Write down what He tells you, then share it with your parents and ask them for help to do it.

QUESTIONS - TEACHERS ANSWER KEY

1. **Why did Jacob have to leave home?**
   Esau wanted to kill him

2. **Who was Jacob going to live with?**
   Uncle Laban

3. **What did Jacob see in his dream?**
   A ladder from heaven with angels

4. **What did he do with the stones he used for a pillow?**
   He built an altar to God and poured oil on it

5. **What did Jacob call the name of the place he had the dream?**
   Bethel

6. **What are the names of Laban's two daughters?**
   Leah and Rachel

7. **What was the name of the woman Jacob met in the field?**
   Rachel

8. **Who was first given to Jacob as his wife?**
   Leah

9. **How many years did Jacob agree to work for Laban?**
   Seven years

10. **What did God say to Jacob in his dream?**
    (Any of these, will be in their own words)
    I am with you.
    I will watch over you wherever you go.
    I will bring you back to this land.
    I will not forsake you until I have done what I promised you.

QUESTIONS - CHILDREN'S COPY

1. Why did Jacob have to leave home?

2. Who was Jacob going to live with?

3. What did Jacob see in his dream?

4. What did he do with the stones he used for a pillow?

5. What did Jacob call the name of the place he had the dream?

6. What are the names of Laban's two daughters?

7. What was the name of the woman Jacob met in the field?

8. Who was given to Jacob as his wife?

9. How many years did Jacob agree to work for him?

10. What did God say to Jacob in his dream?

CRAFTS FOR TORAH PORTION VAYETZE

SUPPLIES:
Popsicle sticks
Cotton Balls
Black card stock
Green construction paper
Plain white paper
White cardstock
Glue/glue stick
Pencils/markers
Gold/silver star stickers

CRAFTS:
Jacob's Ladder Craft

1. On black cardstock, glue with the glue sticks green strips of construction paper on the bottom to represent grass.
2. Glue with the glue popsicle sticks as shown to represent the ladder.

3. Stick star stickers on the sky.
4. Glue with the glue cotton balls on top as shown.

5. Take the pre-cut angels and glue them in various spots on the ladder and night sky.

6. Color sleeping Jacob. Cut him out (some children may need help). Glue him at the bottom of the green stripe.
7. For extra time, color the ladder. You could also decorate it with gems.

THE FINISHED WORK

Vayishlach

"He Sent"

Torah Portion 8:
Vayishlach - He Sent

Scriptures:
Genesis 32:4-36:43, Obadiah 1:1-2, Psalm 140

Vayishlach is the Hebrew word translated as **"sent."** It is found in the first verse of our Torah reading.

Genesis 32:4 TLV
Then Jacob **sent** messengers before him to his brother Esau, to the land of Seir, the field of Edom.

The theme of the Torah Portion:

Family Reunion

Genesis 32:4-7

Then Jacob sent messengers before him to his brother Esau, to the land of Seir, the field of Edom. **5** He also commanded them saying, "This is what you should say to my lord, to Esau: 'This is what your servant Jacob said: I've been staying with Laban, and have lingered until now. **6** Now I've come to possess oxen and donkeys, flocks, male servants and female servants. I sent word to tell my lord, in order to find favor in your eyes.'"

Torah Portion Outline

Genesis Chapter 32:4-32
- Jacob Prepares to Meet Esau, **Gen.32:4-13**
- Jacob Sends Tribute to Esau, **Gen.32:14-24**
- Jacob Wrestles With the Angel, **Gen.32:25-32**

Genesis Chapter 33:1-20
- Jacob Meets Esau, **Gen.33:1-15**
- Jacob and Esau Part Ways, **Gen.33:16-17**
- Jacob Goes to Shechem, **Gen.33:18-20**

Genesis Chapter 34:1-31
- Dinah Defiled by Shechem, **Gen.34:1-5**
- Jacob Tells His Sons About Dinah's Defilement, **Gen.34:6-12**
- The Circumcision Deception, **Gen.34:13-31**

Genesis Chapter 35:1-29
- Rededication at Beth-El, **Gen.35:1-5**
- Death of Rebekah and Deborah, **Gen.35:6-9**
- God Changed Jacob's Name, **Gen.35:10-15**
- Rachel's Death in Childbirth, **Gen.35:16-20**
- Rueben's Error, **Gen.35:21-26**
- Israel (Jacob) Reunites With Isaac, **Gen.35:21-29**

Genesis Chapter 36:1-43
- Esau's Descendants, **Gen.36:1-5**
- Esau Separates From Jacob, **Gen.36:6-19**
- Descendants of Seir, **Gen.36:20-30**
- Kings of Edom, **Gen.36:31-43**

LESSON SUMMARY:

Last week's Torah Portion ended with Jacob leaving his uncle Laban's house to return to his father Isaac in Beer-sheba. This Torah Portion begins with Jacob sending his servants to meet his brother Esau with gifts. He sent Esau goats, camels, lambs, and donkeys.

The servants returned with a message saying that they visited Esau and he was also coming to meet him with four hundred men. Jacob became very fearful because he didn't know why Esau was coming to visit him. He thought Esau wanted revenge for taking his blessing twenty years ago.

Jacob divided all he had, both people and animals, into two camps. He thought if Esau attacks one camp then the other camp can escape. He prayed and asked God for protection. Jacob also prepared an offering for his brother Esau and gave it to the servants in charge of the first camp. He sent them ahead of him and then he stayed with his family in the second camp.

Jacob sent his family across the stream at the brook Jabbok, but he spent the night on the other side of the stream. That night he wrestled with an angel in the form of a man until morning. Jacob said to the man, I will not let you go until you bless me. The man asked him, "What is your name?" He replied, Jacob. The man told him your name will no longer be called Jacob, but it will be Israel.

After he wrestle with the man, Jacob met his brother Esau and the 400 men who were with him. Esau was happy to see his brother and he began to cry, hugged him, and kissed him.

LESSON DISCUSSION:

"DO NOT FEAR"

Jacob was afraid when he heard that Esau was coming to meet him. He was not coming alone but with 400 men. This made Jacob extremely fearful because the last time he saw his brother, Esau threatened to kill him. It had been twenty years since Jacob received the blessing their father Isaac wanted to give to Esau.

Genesis 34:7-9 — The messengers returned to Jacob saying, "We went to your brother, to Esau, and he's also coming out to meet you—and 400 men with him." **8** So Jacob became extremely afraid and distressed. He divided the people with him, along with the flocks and herds and camels, into two camps, **9** for he thought, "If Esau comes to one camp and strikes it, the camp that's left will escape."

Can you imagine what was going through Jacob's mind when he heard that Esau and all those men were coming?

Sometimes when we do things that we shouldn't do, or treat others unkindly, we become fearful because we do not know how that person will react to us.

How do your parents react when you don't do what they tell you to do?

Jacob prayed and asked God to protect him and his family. He also asked God to guide him to do the right thing when he sees his brother Esau. Jacob brought Esau gifts, a peace offering to show kindness to Esau.

Genesis 34:10-13 — **10** Then Jacob said, "O God of my father Abraham, and God of my father Isaac, *Adonai*, who said to me, 'Return to your land and to your relatives and I will do good with you.' **11** I am unworthy of all the proofs of mercy and of all the dependability that you have shown to your servant. For with only my staff I crossed over this Jordan, and now

I've become two camps. **12** Deliver me, please, from my brother's hand, from Esau's hand, for I'm afraid of him that he'll come and strike me—the mothers with the children. **13** You Yourself said, 'I will most certainly do good with you, and will make your seed like the sand of the sea that cannot be counted because of its abundance.'"

Have you ever been afraid of anyone or something? How did you get over your fear?

When you are afraid, like Jacob you too can pray and ask God for protection. If it is someone you are afraid of, ask God to give you the boldness to tell your parents so they can help you.

When God called Joshua to lead the children of Israel to the promised land He told Joshua, "Do not be afraid because I am with you."

As believers in Yeshua, we don't have to be afraid, because He is with us always. We also have the Ruach HaKodesh (Holy Spirit) to pray for us when we do not know how to pray.

Philippians 4:6 NLT — Don't worry about anything; instead, pray about everything. Tell God what you need, and thank him for all he has done.

TURNING POINT:

GOING TO THE WRONG PLACE. GENESIS 34:1-31

Jacob left uncle Laban's place with the intention to go and see his father Isaac in Beersheba, but for some reason, he decided to stop in Shechem and pitched his tent for a while. After some time, his daughter Dinah decided to go see the other girls that were living in Shechem. There was a prince whose name was Shechem. Yes, I know it's weird, he has the same name as the town he lived in. Anyway, Shechem loved Dinah the very first moment he saw her. He was so in love with her, he thought if he didn't have her to be his wife he would die. Shechem could not wait to talk to his father Hamor, or Dinah's father Jacob, to ask to marry her. Shechem, driven by his uncontrolled love for her, took Dinah and had sex with her. This was a big mistake. He should have waited for his father to ask Jacob if he could marry her. He told his father to go and ask Jacob to let her be his wife.

Hamor came to Jacob and told him that his son Shechem loved his daughter and what he did to her. Jacob was silent. He waited until her brothers came home from the field to tell them all that Hamor said. They were very angry, especially Simeon and Levi. They said, "Hamor, your son can marry our sister but only under one condition." All the men in your town must be circumcised like us. This they said deceitfully because they had no intention of letting their sister marry Shechem. Hamor agreed to have all the men circumcised. After three days, when all the men were in pain, Levi and Simeon went throughout the entire town and killed all the men, and took everything they had. When Jacob heard about what they did, he cried and said what have you done to me? You have caused trouble for me in this place. I can no longer live here.

We are not given any specific reason why Jacob decided to stop in Shechem instead of going to Beersheba. However, we can see that his decision not only to stop but to live in Shechem, led to one bad decision to the next. His decision to live there caused Dinah to go looking to see what the other girls were doing. Which eventually led to her brothers killing innocent men.

Every decision we make has consequences. We can make good decisions that have great rewards. We can also make bad decisions that lead to death.

As children, it is always best to obey your parents because they are responsible for you and God will hold them accountable for the choices they make.

It is important not to allow your friends, your interest in things, or places to lead you to make wrong choices. Dinah was interested to know more about the girls. She followed her desire to know and it caused her pain.

Next time someone tries to convince you to go somewhere or do something you are not sure is right, pray and ask the Holy Spirit for wisdom to make the right choice.

Don't allow your desire to know about something, someone, or a strange place to lead you down the wrong path.

PRACTICAL APPLICATIONS

FOR CHILDREN 4-6 YEARS OLD

Ask your parents to help you read and memorize Philippians 4:6

Philippians 4:6 NLT — Don't worry about anything; instead, pray about everything. Tell God what you need, and thank him for all he has done.

FOR CHILDREN 7-12 YEARS OLD

Read and memorize Philippians 4:6

Philippians 4:6 NLT — Don't worry about anything; instead, pray about everything. Tell God what you need, and thank him for all he has done.

Think about something that makes you fearful. Write it down. Pray and ask the Holy Spirit to give you the boldness to share with your parents so they can help you overcome your fear.

FOLLOW-UP FROM THE LAST TORAH PORTION

Ask who wants to share from last week's practical application.

FOR CHILDREN 4-6 YEARS OLD

Ask your parents to show you a picture of a family member you don't know. Ask if you can call and talk with him or her.

FOR CHILDREN 7-12 YEARS OLD

Make a list of three things you want. Ask your heavenly Father if these are His choices for you.

Listen for Him to answer during the week. Write each of His answers next to what you want.

Write about how His answers made you feel.

QUESTIONS - TEACHERS ANSWER KEY

1. **How many men were traveling with Esau?**
   400

2. **Whom did Jacob send to meet his brother Esau?**
   His servants

3. **What was the name of the stream where Jacob wrestled with a man?**
   Jabbok

4. **Why was Jacob afraid of Esau?**
   He thought Esau still wanted to kill him for his blessing

5. **What was the new name Jacob was given?**
   Israel

6. **What did Jacob ask God for when he heard Esau was coming?**
   Protection

7. **What did Esau do when he met Jacob?**
   Cried, hugged him, and kiss him

8. **What did Jacob give Esau as gifts?**
   Goats, lambs, camels, and donkeys

9. **How many children did Jacob have when he left Laban's house?**
   Eleven (11)

10. **What was the name of Jacob's wives?**
    Leah and Rachel

QUESTIONS - CHILDREN'S COPY

1. How many men were traveling with Esau?

2. Whom did Jacob send to meet his brother Esau?

3. What was the name of the stream where Jacob wrestled with a man?

4. Why was Jacob afraid of Esau?

5. What was the new name Jacob was given?

6. What did Jacob ask God for when he heard Esau was coming?

7. What did Esau do when he met Jacob?

8. What did Jacob give Esau as gifts?

9. How many children did Jacob have when he left Laban's house?

10. What was the name of Jacob's wives?

CRAFTS FOR TORAH PORTION VAYISHLACH

SUPPLIES:
White cardstock for letters
Bright color 12"x12" card stock
Plain paper to print the menorah on.
Gold cardstock
Glue stick
Gems
Markers/colored pencils

CRAFTS: "Jacob is now Israel"

1. Distribute large bright-colored large cardstocks to the children.
2. First distribute all letters of the name Jacob, letter by letter, until the children have all the letters. Then with the glue sticks, the children will glue Jacob's name on the paper. They should follow the placement as per the original example.
3. The children will color each letter as they wish.
4. Then distribute 2 gold arrows per child. Let the children glue them facing up as shown in the original.
5. Distribute all 5 Hebrew letters for the word "Yisrael", letter by letter, until children have all the letters. Then the children should follow closely the original for the order and direction of the letters. You could let them know the letters from right to left: Yud, Shin, Reish, Aleph, and Lamed. Glue them with the glue stick. Then color each letter. Decorate each letter with colorful gems. They should be creative and decorate it in the way that they like.
6. At the end, distribute paper menorah. The children will color it and glue it at the bottom in the center as shown.
7. If there's extra time, have the children draw around it or use star stickers, etc to make it even more original to them.

FINAL ARTWORK:

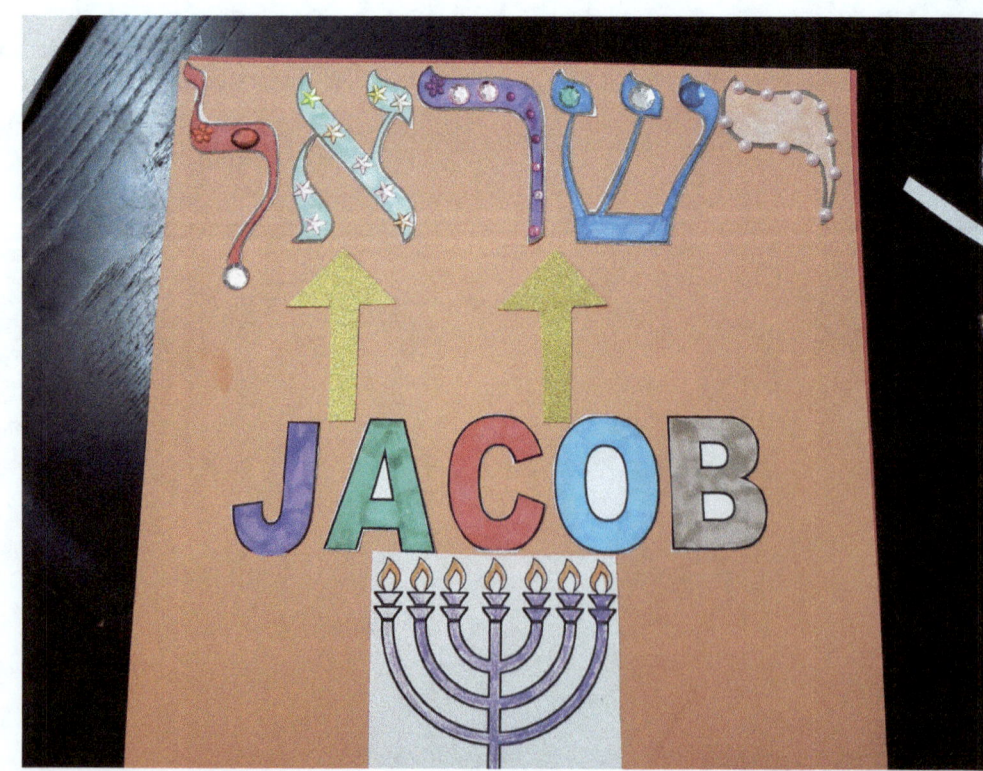

Vayeshev

"He Continued Living"

Torah Portion 9:
Vayeshev - He Lived

Scriptures:
Genesis 37:1-40:23, Psalm 112, Amos 2:6–3:8, Acts 7:9–16

Vayeshev is the Hebrew for "he lived or settled." It is found in the first verse of our Torah reading.

Genesis 37:1 NIV
Jacob lived in the land where his father had stayed, the land of Canaan.

The Theme of the Torah Portion:

The Dreamer

Genesis 37: 9

Then he had another dream, and he told it to his brothers. "Listen," he said, "I had another dream, and this time the sun and moon and eleven stars were bowing down to me."

Torah Portion Outline

Genesis Chapter 37:1-36
- Joseph the Favorite Son, **Gen.37:1-11**
- Joseph Betrayed and Sold, **Gen. 37:12-37**

Genesis Chapter 38:1-27
- Judah and Tamar

Genesis Chapter 39:1-23
- Joseph Success in Potiphar's House, **Gen.39:1-6**
- Joseph Accused of Rape and Imprisoned, **Gen. 39:7-23**

Genesis Chapter 40:1-23
- Joseph Interprets the Dreams of the Baker and Cupbearer

LESSON SUMMARY:

In last week's Torah Portion, we learned of Jacob's fear and struggle as he made his way home to Hebron. Jacob was afraid to meet his brother Esau. God reassured Jacob that he was with him and he should not be afraid. The Torah portion ended with Jacob visiting his father Isaac before he died. Isaac was 180 years old when he died.

After Isaac died, Jacob continued to live in the land where his father lived. In this Torah Portion, we learn about the life of Jacob and his sons in the land. Jacob had twelve sons, but Joseph was his favorite. Jacob made Joseph a very colorful coat.

Joseph's brothers did not love him very much because he brought a bad report of them to their father. They called him the dreamer. Joseph had two dreams about things that would happen in the future. Each time he had a dream he would share it with his brothers and that made them hate him even more. In his first dream, his brothers were bowing down to him. In the second dream, both his parents and his brothers were bowing down to him. This God showed him as a sign of what would happen in the future. Joseph and his brothers did not understand the meaning of the dreams, but Jacob, their father, kept the dreams in his heart.

One day their father sent Joseph to check on his brothers who were out in the field with the animals. Joseph was a good distance away when they recognized him coming. They said to each other "Here comes the dreamer." They plotted to kill Joseph and tell their father that he was killed by a dangerous wild animal. When Reuben, their oldest brother heard their plot, he said to them don't kill him, just throw him in a pit in the field. He said this because he wanted to rescue Joseph from his brothers who wanted to kill him. They all agreed and threw Joseph in a pit. Afterward, they saw a caravan of Ishmaelites coming from Gilead carrying different spices, herbs, and fruits to Egypt. When Judah saw that they were merchants who buy and sell goods and slaves, he said to his brothers, let us sell Joseph because killing him will not benefit us. They sold Joseph to the merchants for twenty pieces of silver. Joseph was then sold to Potiphar the captain of Pharaoh's bodyguards.

LESSON DISCUSSION:

JOSEPH, A SLAVE IN EGYPT

Joseph was Jacob's favorite son, and all his brothers knew it. Giving Joseph a special coat of many colors did not help Joseph either. Joseph was hated by his brothers, they didn't even want to speak to him.

Can you imagine being hated by your brother or sister and he/she will not talk with you unless your parents tell them to? Or do you hate anyone and cannot talk with him/her?

Hate and murder separate us from God.
Joseph's brothers hated him so much that they wanted to kill him. Did you know that if you hate someone, it is just like you killed that person?

1 John 3:15 CEB — Everyone who hates a brother or sister is a murderer, and you know that murderers don't have eternal life residing in them.

God did not love the hate that Joseph's brothers showed toward him, but He still loved them. God had a plan for Joseph's life and He showed it to him in dreams. God allowed Joseph to be sold by his brothers.

Why would God allow something that terrible to happen?
God is in control but He does not control our choices. He has the power to use the choices we make to work together so His purpose can be accomplished. God used what Joseph's brothers did to him for His purpose. We will learn in the future, that while Joseph was in Egypt there was a severe famine, and there was no food. God used Joseph to help save his entire family and the people in Egypt. Joseph met his brothers in Egypt and they were afraid because they thought he would punish them for what they did to him. He told them; "You intended to harm me, but God intended it for good to accomplish what is now being done, the saving of many lives." Genesis 50:20

Have you had a dream but you could not remember it when you were awake? Or don't know the meaning of a dream you had?

God is the giver of dreams and He will also give us the meaning of our dreams. Pray and ask the Holy Spirit to help you remember your dreams and to tell you what they mean.

God has a plan for your life. You might not know what His plan is right now, but you can ask Him and He will show it to you.

Remember God does not control your choices but it is always best to make choices that will please Him.

TURNING POINT:

REMEMBER ME!

God prepared Joseph through dreams of what would happen to him in the future and also gave him the gift of interpreting dreams that would help him while he was in Egypt. Interpreting dreams is a gift from God. Joseph was able to use this gift while he was living in Egypt; he still felt like he was forgotten. He was away from his family feeling unloved and abandoned.

Although Joseph was sold as a slave in Egypt God was with him and he was favored by the captain of Pharaoh's bodyguards, Potiphar, who bought him from the Ishmaelites. One day Pharaoh was angry with his chief cupbearer and chief baker so he sent them to Potiphar to put them in prison. It was the same place where Joseph was. The commander of the prison put Joseph in charge of them.

Genesis 40:2-4 — **2** Pharaoh was angry with his two officials, with the chief of the cupbearers and with the chief of the bakers. **3** So he put them in custody of the house of the commander of the bodyguards—in the prison, the place where Joseph was confined. **4** The commander of the bodyguards assigned Joseph to be with them and served them as their personal servant. They were in custody for some time.

While in prison both men had a dream the same night. In the morning they were very troubled because they did not understand their dreams, and they could not find anyone who could (interpret) tell them the meaning of the dreams either. God gave Joseph the meaning of Pharaoh's cupbearer and chief baker's dreams.

Genesis 40:5-8 — **5** Then the two of them each dreamed a dream on the same night. The dream of each man—the cupbearer and the baker of the king of Egypt, who were confined in the prison—each had its own interpretation. **6** When Joseph came to them in the morning, he observed them, and there they were, looking miserable. **7** So he asked Pharaoh's officials who were with him in the custody of the house of his master saying, "Why are your faces so sad today?" **8** They said to him, "We dreamed a dream and there is no one to interpret it."Then Joseph said to them, "Don't interpretations belong to God? Please tell me."

Joseph Interprets the dreams of the cupbearer and the baker. He told the cupbearer, in another three days, Pharaoh will lift your head and restore you to your position. Then you'll put Pharaoh's cup in his hand just as you used to do before when you were his cupbearer. But if you remember me, that I was with you, when it goes well with you, please show me kindness and mention me to Pharaoh and get me out of this house. For I was forcibly kidnapped from the land of the Hebrews, and even here I have done nothing at all that they should put me in this pit." **Genesis 40:13-15**

In three days the king did just as Joseph told the cupbearer. The King gave him back his job and he served the king, but he did not remember Joseph.

Joseph was in the place where God wanted him. It was in Egypt that God would use Joseph to save his family. Joseph did not feel loved and he surely did not want to be in prison. He did not know yet God's purpose for him. He felt abandoned and forgotten.

Have you ever felt abandoned and forgotten? God remembers you even when no one does. His promise is never to leave you or turn His back on you. Even when there is no one to say "I love you' remember your Heavenly Father loves you.

PRACTICAL APPLICATIONS:
SHOW KINDNESS INSTEAD OF HATE

FOR CHILDREN 4-6 YEARS OLD
Be kind to your brother/sister even when it is hard.

If you don't have a brother or sister, ask your parents if you can share your lunch with a friend or a neighbor.

FOR CHILDREN 7-12 YEARS OLD
Be intentional about telling your parents and friends that you love them.

Look for ways you can show love to someone who is not your friend at school and that you love him/her. **Example:** share lunch, be kind when everyone else is mean, help your teacher carry her books

FOLLOW-UP FROM THE LAST TORAH PORTION
Ask who wants to share from last week's practical application

FOR CHILDREN 4-6 YEARS OLD
Ask your parents to help you read and memorize Philippians 4:6

Philippians 4:6 NLT — Don't worry about anything; instead, pray about everything. Tell God what you need, and thank him for all he has done.

FOR CHILDREN 7-12 YEARS OLD

Read and memorize Philippians 4:6
Philippians 4:6 NLT — Don't worry about anything; instead, pray about everything. Tell God what you need, and thank Him for all he has done.

Think about something that makes you fearful. Write it down. Pray and ask the Holy Spirit to give you the boldness to share with your parents so they can help you overcome your fear.

QUESTIONS - TEACHERS ANSWER KEY

1. How many sons did Jacob have?
12

2. How old was Isaac when he died?
180 years old

3. Who was Jacob's favorite son?
Joseph

4. What is the name of the place Jacob lived?
Hebron

5. What did Jacob give to Joseph?
A coat of many colors

6. Whose idea was it to put Joseph in a pit?
Reuben

7. Whose idea was it to sell Joseph?
Judah

8. Who were the merchants that bought Joseph?
Ishmaelites

9. To Which country was Joseph sold?
Egypt

10. What is the name of the man who bought Joseph in Egypt?
Potiphar

11. What two officials were put in prison with Joseph?
Cupbearer and baker

QUESTIONS - CHILDREN'S COPY

1. How many sons did Jacob have?

2. How old was Isaac when he died?

3. Who was Jacob's favorite son?

4. What is the name of the place Jacob lived?

5. What did Jacob give to Joseph?

6. Whose idea was it to put Joseph in a pit?

7. Whose idea was it to sell Joseph?

8. Who were the merchants that bought Joseph?

9. To Which country was Joseph sold?

10. What is the name of the man who bought Joseph in Egypt?

11. What two officials were put in prison with Joseph?

CRAFTS FOR TORAH PORTION VAYESHEV

SUPPLIES:
1. Brown construction paper
2. Colorful construction paper
3. Colorful cardstock paper
4. Scissors
5. Glue and glue sticks
6. Small Doll plastic eyes
7. Color pencils/markers to draw the nose, mouth, and hair
8. Popsicle sticks

CRAFTS: JOSEPH IN A COAT OF MANY COLORS.

1. Children will receive cut-outs of the Joseph Paper doll.
2. Children will receive cut-outs of Joseph's t-shirt and shorts.
3. Have the students glue the shirt and shorts on a paper doll.

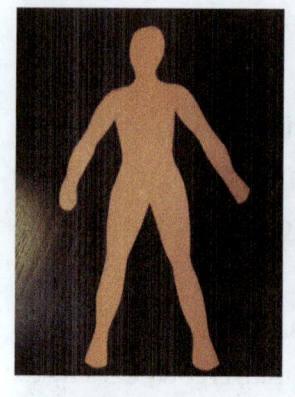

4. Children will receive cut-outs of the front (2 panels) and back of the coat (color varies!)

5. Have the children first glue the back of the coat.
6. Then the 2 panels of the front, match it to the back!

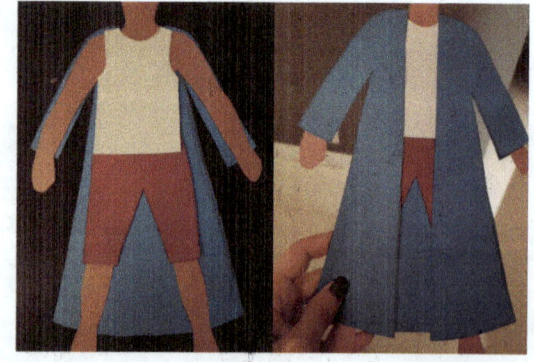

7. Children will receive the back side of Joseph's head.
8. Have them glue it to the back of his head.
9. With a black pencil or marker, draw the hair on his forehead and sides.
10. Then the children should paste on the doll's eyes.
11. Draw in the nose and mouth. Draw the sandals.
12. There will be a big bag of colorful cut-out strips. Have the children grab a handful of the strips and paste them on the back and the front of the coat.

13. Then the last touch is to take a popsicle stick and glue it at the bottom as shown.

NOW THE CHILDREN HAVE THEIR OWN JOSEPH PAPER DOLL!

Mikeitz

"At The End"

Torah Portion 10:
Mikeitz - At The End

Scriptures:
Genesis 41:1-44:17, 1 Kings 3:15–4:1, Acts 7:9–16, Psalm 40

Mikeitz is the Hebrew word for "***at the end***" which is found in the first verse of our Torah portion.

Genesis 41:1 NASB
Now it happened ***at the end*** of two full years that Pharaoh had a dream, and behold, he was standing by the Nile.

The Theme of the Torah Portion:
God's Divine Plan

Genesis 41:38-39

38 Then Pharaoh said to his servants, "Can we find a man like this, in whom there is a divine spirit?" **39** So Pharaoh said to Joseph, "Since God has informed you of all this, there is no one as discerning and wise as you are.

Torah Portion Outline

Genesis 40:1-57 - Pharaoh's Dream and the Interpretation
- Pharaoh's Dreams No One Could Interpret, **Gen.41:1-8**
- Cupbearer Tells Pharaoh About Joseph, **Gen.41:9-13**
- Joseph Interprets Pharaoh's Dreams, **Gen.41:14-31**
- Joseph gave Pharaoh a Strategy, **Gen.41:32-57**

Genesis 42:1-38 - Joseph's brothers come to Egypt to buy food
- Joseph Accused Them of Being Spies, **Gen.42:1-13**
- Joseph Takes Simeon, **Gen.42:14-28**
- Telling Jacob What Happened in Egypt, **Gen.42:29-38**

Genesis 43:1-34 The Return to Egypt
- The Brothers Refuse to Return to Egypt Without Benjamin, **Gen.43:1-11**
- When Joseph Sees Benjamin, **Gen.43:12-17**
- Joseph Has Dinner With His Brothers, **Gen.43:18-34**

Genesis 44:1-34 The Silver Cup and Judah's plea
- Josephs Plot to Keep Benjamin, **Gen.44:1-13**
- Judah Pleads For Benjamin to Return Home, **Gen.44:13-34**

LESSON SUMMARY:

At the end of two years, after Joseph interpreted the dreams for Pharaoh's cupbearer and baker, Pharaoh had two dreams that made him fearful. He called all his magicians, the wise men, and the fortune tellers of Egypt, he told them his dreams but no one could tell him the meaning of his dreams. Pharaoh was deeply troubled by these dreams that no one could interpret. Then the cupbearer said to Pharaoh, remember the time when you threw me in prison because I didn't do my job the right way? There was a Hebrew boy whom Potiphar had in the prison, he was in charge. Both I and your chief baker had dreams one night but we didn't know what they meant. The Hebrew boy, Joseph told us the meaning of our dreams and it happened just the way he said it would. He told me I would serve you again, but for the chief baker, things didn't turn out well for him.

Pharaoh sent for Joseph. When Joseph came to Pharaoh's palace, Pharaoh said to Joseph, I had a dream, but no one can tell me the meaning. My cupbearer told me you can interpret dreams. Joseph answered Pharaoh, God is the one who gives the meaning of dreams, it has nothing to do with me. So Pharaoh then told his dreams to Joseph. He said, "In my dream, there I was, standing on the bank of the Nile; and I saw, seven cows, fat and fine-looking came up out of the Nile, and they grazed in the marsh grass. Then I saw, seven other cows came up after them, poor and very ugly and thin, such ugliness I have never seen in all the land of Egypt; the thin and ugly cows ate the first seven fat cows. After they had eaten them, you could not tell because they were thin and ugly as before. Then I awoke. I went back to sleep and I saw also in another dream, seven ears of grain, full and good, came up on a single stalk; and, seven ears, withered, thin, and scorched by the east wind sprouted up after them; and the thin ears swallowed the seven good ears. Then I told it to the fortune tellers and magicians, but no one could explain it to me." **Genesis 41:15-24 NASB2020**

Joseph told Pharaoh that God had shown him things that are about to happen. He told Pharaoh, the two dreams are the same, and that God showed them to him twice because it is important. Joseph told Pharaoh that the seven cows and the seven grains represent seven years. The fat cow and the good grain are seven years of plenty of food and a great harvest. The seven thin cows and withered grain represents seven years of famine and no food. The famine will be great so that no one will remember the seven years of plenty. Joseph not only told Pharaoh the meaning of his dream, but also a way to preserve food during the seven years of plenty that would last until the seven years of famine were over. Pharaoh was pleased with Joseph's idea to store food for seven years. He made Joseph ruler of Egypt and put him in charge of all he had to make sure everything that Joseph told him would be done. Joseph became the second-greatest ruler in Egypt. Only Pharaoh was more powerful than him. Joseph received gifts of fine linen garments, a gold necklace, Pharaoh's signet ring of authority, and he was also given a wife whose name was Asenath. She was the daughter of Potiphera, the priest of On. Joseph was thirty years old when he was made ruler of Egypt.

During the seven years of plenty, the land of Egypt produced great harvests. Joseph built storehouses in every city next to the fields and collected food from everyone. The amount of food he collected was too much for him to count. Joseph's wife had two sons before the seven years of famine began. Joseph named the firstborn, Manasseh; "For," he said, "God has made me forget all my trouble and all of my father's household." And he named the second Ephraim; "For," he said, "God has made me fruitful in the land of my affliction." **Genesis 41:51-52**

When the seven years of famine began Joseph opened the storehouses and all the people in Egypt and other nations came to Joseph to buy food. Even Joseph's brothers came to Egypt to buy food, but they did not recognize him because he spoke to them in the Egyptian language and had someone translate what he said into Hebrew to them.

LESSON DISCUSSION:

GOD'S PROMOTION

God used Joseph to interpret Pharaoh's dream and also to promote him as a ruler in Egypt. Joseph became the second most powerful man in all of Egypt. His life was changed. He went from being a slave in prison to the only person Pharaoh would take advice from.

Do you remember what Joseph told the chief cupbearer in last week's Torah portion after he told him the interpretation of his dream? (Allow children to answer)
He told him to remember me. Tell Pharaoh about me so I can get out of this prison.

Genesis 40:14-15
Only keep me in mind when it goes well for you, and please do me a kindness by mentioning me to Pharaoh, and get me out of this prison. **15** For I was in fact kidnapped from the land of the Hebrews, and even here I have done nothing that they should have put me into the dungeon."

The cupbearer did not remember Joseph until Pharaoh had his dream and could not find anyone to tell him the meaning.

It seemed a little selfish that the cupbearer did not remember Joseph, but God did not want Joseph to depend on anyone to promote him because He had a specific job for Joseph.

God also wanted Joseph to learn to trust Him and know that He was in control even though he was a slave in prison.

Psalm 75:5 Voice There is no one *on earth* who can raise up another *to grant honor,* not from the east or the west, not from the desert. *There is no one. God is the only One.*

You and I may not be slaves in a prison, but when we spend more time with things than we do with God we can become slaves to them.

What are some of the things you have that you love to spend time playing with? Or friends that you love talking with?

Do you spend more time with these things or friends than you spend time talking with God or reading about God?

God has a specific job for each of us.
God, our heavenly Father, also had a specific job for Yeshua.
God loves us and He wants to have a relationship with us, but because of sin, we cannot have a relationship with Him. God sent Yeshua, as a sacrificial lamb to die so we can put our trust in Him and have a relationship with our Father in heaven. God raised Yeshua from the dead. He is now in heaven with the Father, but the Ruach HaKodesh (the Holy Spirit) is with us on earth to teach us how to have a relationship with our heavenly Father.

Do you believe that God has a specific job for you?
Even though you don't know what that job is right now, it is important to learn to trust God and ask the Holy Spirit to teach you how to have a relationship with Him.

TURNING POINT:

STRANGE PLACES

How would you feel if your brother or sister left you at the park and you did not know how to find your way home? Scared, right? I believe that is how Joseph felt being in a strange place where he knew no one. Joseph missed being home and his family. That is why after he told the cupbearer the meaning of his dream, he said to the cupbearer to tell Pharaoh about him. The cupbearer did not remember Joseph.

God had a plan for Joseph's life and he did not want anyone to say I made Joseph famous. There was also an important lesson for Joseph to learn. Do you remember the dream Joseph had? How he saw the sun, the moon, and the stars bowing down to him? These all represented his father, mother, and also his brothers. Joseph had to learn that when the time came for his father and brothers to bow down to him, it was not because he was better than them but because God used him for a specific job.

Genesis 41:25, 32-36 And Joseph said to Pharaoh, "Pharaoh's dreams are one *and the same*; God has told to Pharaoh what He is about to do. **32** Now as for the repeating of the dream to Pharaoh twice, *it means* that the matter is confirmed by God, and God will quickly bring it about. **33** So now let Pharaoh look for a man discerning and wise, and appoint him over the land of Egypt. **34** Let Pharaoh take action to appoint overseers in charge of the land, and let him take a fifth *of the produce* of the land of Egypt *as a tax* in the seven years of abundance. **35** Then have them collect all the food of these good years that are coming, and store up the grain for food in the cities under Pharaoh's authority, and have them guard *it*. **36** Let the food be *used* as a reserve for the land for the seven years of famine which will occur in the land of Egypt, so that the land will not perish during the famine."

In this week's Torah portion, God used Joseph to tell Pharaoh the meaning of his dreams and also how to make preparations for the future. God showed Pharaoh that there will be seven years of abundance in the land. Afterward, there would also be seven years of famine. The famine would be so bad, no one would remember the seven years of abundance that came before it.

Pharaoh said to Joseph; You shall be in charge of my house, and all my people shall be obedient to you; only *regarding* the throne will I be greater than you." Pharaoh also said to Joseph, "See, I have placed you over all the land of Egypt." **Genesis 41:40-41**

God used Pharaoh's dreams to promote Joseph so that when the famine came and his father and brothers needed food, he would be able to provide for them.

When Joseph's brothers came to buy food in Egypt they did not recognize him, but he recognized them. When his brothers bowed before him Joseph remembered his dreams. "Joseph remembered the dreams which he [had about them, and he said to them, "You are spies; you have come to look at the undefended parts of our land." And they said to him, "No, my lord, but your servants have come to buy food." **Genesis 42:9-10**

Joseph seeing his brothers bowing before him, finally understood the purpose of the dreams he had and why God allowed him to be sold as a slave in Egypt.

You might not understand everything your parents tell you to do but one day you will. God is using them to teach you obedience to Him. Be patient. God has great plans for your life.

PRACTICAL APPLICATIONS
DEMONSTRATING FORGIVENESS

FOR CHILDREN 4-6 YEARS OLD

Give your parents or siblings a hug and kiss when they do something that hurts your feelings.

FOR CHILDREN 7-12 YEARS OLD

Practice forgiveness. Learn to forgive others even when it is hard.

FOLLOW-UP FROM THE LAST TORAH PORTION
Ask who wants to share from last week's practical application.

SHOW KINDNESS INSTEAD OF HATE

FOR CHILDREN 4-6 YEARS OLD
Be kind to your brother/sister even when it is hard.

If you don't have a brother or sister. Ask your parents if you can share your lunch with a friend or a neighbor.

FOR CHILDREN 7-12 YEARS OLD
Be intentional about telling your parents and friends that you love them.

Look for ways you can show love to someone who is not your friend at school and that you love him/her. **Example:** share lunch, be kind when everyone else is mean, and help your teacher carry his/her books.

QUESTIONS - TEACHERS ANSWER KEY

1. **Where was Pharaoh standing in his dreams?**
   By the Nile

2. **How many years was it after Joseph interpreted the cupbearer's dream?**
   Two (2) years

3. **What did Pharaoh see in his first dream?**
   7 fat cows and 7 skinny cows. Skinny cows eat the fat cows

4. **What did Pharaoh see in his second dream?**
   7 good grains and 7 thin grains. Thin grains swallowed good grains

5. **What did the seven fat cows and the seven good grains represent?**
   7 years of plenty/abundance

6. **Who was able to tell Pharaoh the meaning of his dreams?**
   Joseph

7. **What did the seven skinny cows and thin grains represent?**
   7 years of famine

8. **What was the name of Joseph's wife?**
   Asenath

9. **What items did Pharaoh give to Joseph?**
   Signet ring, fine linen garments, gold necklace

10. **What was the name of Joseph's two sons?**
    Manasseh and Ephraim

11. **How old was Joseph when he became a ruler in Egypt?**
    37 years old

QUESTIONS - CHILDREN'S COPY

1. Where was Pharaoh standing in his dreams?

2. How many years was it after Joseph interpreted the cupbearer's dream?

3. What did Pharaoh see in his first dream?

4. What did Pharaoh see in his second dream?

5. What did the seven fat cows and the seven good grains represent?

6. Who was able to tell Pharaoh the meaning of his dreams?

7. What did the seven skinny cows and thin grains represent?

8. What was the name of Joseph's wife?

9. What items did Pharaoh give to Joseph?

10. What was the name of Joseph's two sons?

11. How old was Joseph when he became a ruler in Egypt?

CRAFTS FOR TORAH PORTION MIKEITZ

SUPPLIES:
1. Color cardstock of various colors
2. White cardstock
3. Pink construction paper
4. Black construction paper
5. Black pipe cleaners
6. Plastic doll eyes
7. Glue sticks

CRAFTS: PHARAOH'S DREAM

1. Children will receive cutouts of fat and skinny cows' heads.

2. Children will then receive pink noses for both cows. They will glue it on the appropriate spots.

3. The children will receive pre-cut bodies for both cows and glue the heads to the bodies.

4. Then they will receive pre-cut legs for both cows and glue them in the appropriate spots.

5. The children will receive pre-cut udders (nipples) for both cows and will glue them in the appropriate spots.

6. The children will receive 7 pieces of pre-cut black construction paper for spots. They don't need to follow exactly as the original artwork. They could paste it as they wish.

7. The children will receive pre-cut and pre-curled pipe cleaners and glue them as tails on a fat cow.

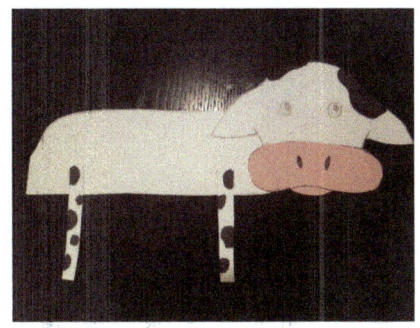

8. Then they will receive large doll eyes and stick them on both cows.

9. Finally, the children will glue both cows on the card stock.

Vayigash

"He Approached"

Torah Portion 11:
Vayigash - He Approached

Scriptures:
Genesis 44:18-47:27, Ezekiel 37:15-28,
Acts 7-9-16, Psalm 48

Vayigash is the Hebrew word for "***he approached***" which is found in the first verse of our Torah portion.

Genesis 44:18 NASB
Then ***Judah approached*** him and said, "Oh my lord, may your servant please speak a word in my lord's ears, and do not be angry with your servant; for you are equal to Pharaoh.

The theme of the Torah Portion:
Chosen by God

Genesis 45:7 TLV
God sent me ahead of you to ensure a remnant in the land and to keep you alive for a great escape.

Torah Portion Outline

Genesis 44:18-34
- Judah Pleads for Benjamin, **Gen.18:34**

Genesis 45:18-28
- Joseph Reveals Himself to His Brothers, **Gen.45:1-16**
- Pharaoh Meets Joseph's Brothers, **Gen.45:17-24**
- Jacob Hears that Joseph is Alive, **Gen.45:25-28**

Genesis 46:1-37
- Jacob Goes to Egypt

Genesis 47:1-27
- Jacob Blessed Pharaoh, **Gen.47:1-13**
- Jacob the Leader, **Gen.47:14-27**

LESSON SUMMARY:

In last week's Torah Portion God used Joseph to interpret Pharaoh's dreams and gave him a plan to prepare for the seven years of famine that was coming. Joseph became a powerful ruler in Egypt. During the seven years of abundance, Joseph built storehouses to store up the food for the seven years of famine. During the famine, Jacob heard that there was food in Egypt so he sent his sons, Joseph's older brothers, to buy food. When they came to Egypt to buy food, they bowed down to Joseph just as he saw in his dream when he was younger. His brothers did not recognize him, but Joseph knew who they were.

Joseph questioned his brothers because he wanted to know if his father and younger brother Benjamin, were still alive. Wanting to see his brother, Benjamin, Joseph pretended they were spies and said to his older brothers, you have to prove to me you are not spies. Return to your home and bring your youngest brother to me. Joseph took his brother Simeon from them and tied him up. He told them if they don't bring Benjamin back, he would keep Simeon in prison. When they returned home and told Jacob all that happened, Jacob was very distressed and angry. He did not want to let Benjamin go. It took a very long time for them to convince Jacob that if he didn't let them take Benjamin with them back to Egypt they could not go to buy food.

When they returned to Egypt with Benjamin, Joseph had his brothers brought to his house. He also took Simeon out of prison and had him brought to his house. Joseph had his servants prepare a meal for him and his brothers. The brothers were very afraid because they did not know why Joseph brought them to his house. They thought it was because they were being punished for selling Joseph. When Joseph came home and saw all his brothers, he became very emotional and wanted to cry. He went into a private room and cried, then he washed his face and came back to have dinner with his brothers. He gave Benjamin five times more food than he gave his other brothers.

Joseph struggled with his emotions and how to reveal himself to his brothers. He was struggling to find a way to tell them. In this week's Torah portion, Joseph reveals himself to his brothers.

LESSON DISCUSSION: ROLE-PLAY

THE GREAT REVEAL

Narrator (Teacher): Joseph wanted to test his brothers to see if they had a change of heart. If they had learned how to love each other since the time they sold him as a slave. Joseph said to one of his servants. Take my silver goblet and put it in Benjamin's bag with food. The servant did as Joseph said. Early the next morning Joseph's brothers left Egypt to return home. Not long after the brothers left, Joseph said to his servants go after them, when you catch up to them say to them; "why have you repay evil for good, taking my master's cup from which he drinks? He even uses it especially to discern by divination." They said to him, "why would we do such a thing?" The money we found in our bags the first time we came to buy food, we returned. Whoever stole silver or gold from your master's house, let him die, and the rest of us will be your slaves. The servant searched everyone's bags, beginning with the oldest to the youngest, and the cup was found in Benjamin's bag. When they saw the cup, they all cried and tore their clothes. Then they returned to Joseph's house with the servant. When Judah and all the brothers entered Joseph's house, they all bowed before him. Judah said, "God has exposed our guilt for selling our brother Joseph. Let us all be your slaves, even the one with whom you found the cup." Joseph replied; "No, not so. The one with whom the cup was found will be my slave."

Judah: Please listen to your servant and don't be angry with me, since you are as powerful as Pharaoh. You asked us if you have a father or brother, and we said yes. He is very old and our youngest brother was born in his old age. Now his brother is dead, so he is the only one of his mother's children left, and his father loves him.' You asked us to bring him down to Egypt so you could look at him and prove we are not spies so we can buy food. We didn't want to bring him, because if anything happened to him we knew it would kill our father. But you were persistent and warned us if we do not bring him, don't come back. We brought the boy with us and now we cannot return home without him, because our father will surely die. So I am begging please take me instead of my brother Benjamin so that my father will not see the death of my father.

Joseph: Get everyone away from me. *(Pretend to cry)*

Joseph: (Take the mask off and say...) I am Joseph, your brother. Is my father still alive?

Narrator (Teacher): The brothers looked scared and could not answer.

Joseph: "Please come near me and give me a hug." "I'm Joseph, your brother—the one you sold to Egypt,". Now, don't be sorrowful, and don't be angry with yourself because you sold me here. There have been two years of famine in the land, and there will be five more years with no harvesting. But God sent me ahead of you to ensure a remnant in the land and to keep you alive for a great escape. It wasn't you, you didn't send me here, but God! And He made me as a father to Pharaoh, lord over his whole house, and ruler over the entire land of Egypt. Go now to my father and tell him I am alive and bring him back to me. (Genesis 45:4-9)

Narrator (Teacher):
When Pharaoh heard that Joseph's brothers were in Egypt. Pharaoh said to Joseph; "Say to your brothers, load your donkeys and go to the land of Canaan, and take your father and your families and come to me; and I will give you the best of the land of Egypt, and you will eat the fat of the land.' Now you are ordered, 'Do this: take wagons from the land of Egypt for your little ones and your wives, and bring your father and come. And do not concern yourselves with your property, for the best of all the land of Egypt is yours.'" (Genesis 45:17-20)

Joseph's brothers did just as Pharaoh commanded them. They returned home to Canaan and told Jacob, their father, all that happened to them while they were in Egypt. When they told him all the words of Joseph that he had spoken to them, and when he saw the wagons that Joseph had sent to carry him, then the spirit of their father Jacob revived. Then Israel said, "It is enough; my son Joseph is still alive. I will go and see him before I die." (Genesis 45:27-28)

TURNING POINT:

LAYOVER IN BEERSHEBA

Joseph sent his brothers home with gifts and wagons for Jacob and the rest of their family to travel to Egypt. Then the brothers returned home to Canaan, and told Jacob that Joseph was alive; they told Jacob that Joseph was alive and he was a ruler in Egypt, but he did not believe them at first. It wasn't until they told him all that Joseph said that he saw the wagons and gifts that were sent for him.

Jacob was excited to know that Joseph was alive and he wanted to go and see him. "I'm convinced! My son Joseph is still alive. I will go and see him before I die."- Genesis 45:28 NIV

On the way down to Egypt, Jacob had a layover, stopping in Beersheba. Beersheba is a place of prayer and covenant. While in Beersheba Jacob prayed and offered a sacrifice to God. God visited Jacob in a vision in the night and reminded him that He (God) is with him.

So Israel set out with all that was his, and when he reached Beersheba, he offered sacrifices to the God of his father Isaac. **2** And God spoke to Israel in a vision at night and said, "Jacob! Jacob!" "Here I am," he replied. **3** "I am God, the God of your father," he said. "Do not be afraid to go down to Egypt, for I will make you into a great nation there. **4** I will go down to Egypt with you, and I will surely bring you back again. And Joseph's own hand will close your eyes. "**5** Then Jacob left Beersheba, and Israel's sons took their father Jacob and their children and their wives in the carts that Pharaoh had sent to transport him. **6** So Jacob and all his offspring went to Egypt, taking with them their livestock and the possessions they had acquired in Canaan. **7** Jacob brought with him to Egypt his sons and grandsons and his daughters and granddaughters—all his offspring. Genesis 46-7 NIV

Wait a minute!! When did Jacob say he was afraid to go down to Egypt? The Torah does not tell us that Jacob was afraid, but God is all-knowing and all-powerful. He knew what was in Jacob's heart.

Going to new places can be exciting and scary at the same time. Jacob was excited to see Joseph, his son whom he thought was dead all these years. At the same time, he was afraid because he did not know what life would be like in Egypt.

Sometimes we are afraid like Jacob to go to new places because we do not know what to expect. God told Jacob that he did not need to be afraid because He (God) is with him. Not only was God with Jacob, but He promised to make him into a great nation while he was in Egypt. God also promised to bring Jacob up from Egypt, just as he had promised Abraham.

We too have the same promise. God will not leave us! Yeshua said, He will be with us always even until the end of the world, (Matthew 28:20). When you don't understand God's plan or why your parents decide to move to a new place, you don't have to worry. You can have your own Beersheba layover in prayer. You can pray and ask God to give you wisdom and understanding and He will.

James 1:5 NIV
If any of you lacks wisdom, you should ask God, who gives generously to all without finding fault, and it will be given to you.

PRACTICAL APPLICATIONS
DEMONSTRATING THE SPIRIT OF TRUTH

FOR CHILDREN 4-6 YEARS OLD

Always tell your parents the truth, even when you are afraid of getting in trouble.

FOR CHILDREN 7-12 YEARS OLD

Telling your friends the truth sometimes can hurt their feelings. Ask the Holy Spirit to teach you how to speak the truth in love and with kindness.

FOLLOW-UP FROM THE LAST TORAH PORTION

Ask who wants to share from last week's practical application.

PRACTICAL APPLICATIONS
DEMONSTRATING FORGIVENESS

FOR CHILDREN 4-6 YEARS OLD

Give your parents or siblings a hug and kiss when they do something that hurts your feelings.

FOR CHILDREN 7-12 YEARS OLD

Practice forgiveness. Learn to forgive others even when it is hard.

QUESTIONS - TEACHERS ANSWER KEY

1. **What is the name of Joseph's younger brother?**
   Benjamin

2. **Which brother was put in prison by Joseph?**
   Simeon

3. **Where did Joseph meet his brothers when they came back to Egypt?**
   At his house

4. **How many more servings of food did Benjamin receive than his other brothers?**
   Five (5) times more

5. **What did Joseph tell his servant to put in his brothers' bag?**
   His silver goblet (cup)

6. **In whose bag did the servant put the silver goblet (cup)?**
   Benjamin

7. **Which brother wanted to take Benjamin's place as Joseph's slave?**
   Judah

8. **What animal did they use to carry the gifts and wagons to Jacob?**
   Donkey

9. **Who sent gifts to Jacob?**
   Pharaoh

10. **What was Joseph's big secret?**
    He was their brother

11. **Who did Joseph say sent him to Egypt and why?**
    God, to save them during the famine

QUESTIONS - CHILDREN'S COPY

1. What is the name of Joseph's younger brother?

2. Which brother was put in prison by Joseph?

3. Where did Joseph meet his brothers when they came back to Egypt?

4. How many more servings of food did Benjamin receive than his other brothers?

5. What did Joseph tell his servant to put in his brothers' bag?

6. In whose bag did the servant put the silver goblet (cup)?

7. Which brother wanted to take Benjamin's place as Joseph's slave?

8. What animal did they use to carry the gifts and wagons to Jacob?

9. Who sent gifts to Jacob?

10. What was Joseph's big secret?

11. Who did Joseph say sent him to Egypt and why?

CRAFTS FOR TORAH PORTION VAYIGASH

SUPPLIES:
1. Brown cardstock paper
2. Black construction paper
3. Black and red pencils
4. Gold foil paper
5. Various colors of card stock paper
6. Colorful Gems and studs
7. Popsicle Sticks
8. Glue sticks
9. Few rolls of Scotch Tape (please kindly provide)

CRAFTS: JOSEPH'S MASK:

1. Children will receive pre-cut brown cardstock masks.
2. They will also receive pre-cut eyeliner and eyebrows.
3. With the glue sticks, they will glue eyeliner and eyebrows as indicated.
4. With pencils, they will draw noses nostrils, and lips.

5. They will also receive a gold foil thick stripe to glue across.
6. Then they will receive colorful headpieces. With the scotch tape, they will attach it. Use the original mask as an example.

7. Now, decorate: With already pre-cut gold foil strips, the children will glue some vertically at the top of the headpiece, and 1 on each end. Then, by using gems and studs, they could decorate the headpieces as they wish. Creativity is welcomed!
8. Attach 2 popsicle sticks at the bottom of the mask. Then use it for the "Joseph Reveals Himself to Brothers" skit.

Vayechi

"He Lived"

Torah Portion 12:

Vayechi - He Lived

Scriptures:

Genesis 47:28-50:26, 1Kings 2:1-12, Hebrews 11:21-22, 1Peter 1:3-9, Psalm 41

Vayechi is the Hebrew word for "***he lived***" which is found in the first verse of our Torah portion.

Genesis 47:28 TLV

Now ***Jacob lived*** in the land of Egypt for 17 years, so the days of Jacob, the years of his life, were 147 years.

The Theme of the Torah Portion:
Family Legacy-The Blessing

Genesis 49:1
Jacob called his sons and said to them: Gather together so that I can tell you what will happen to you in the last days.

Genesis 48:15-16

15 Then he blessed Joseph and said, "The God before whom my fathers Abraham and Isaac walked, The God who has shepherded me throughout my life to this day, **16** The Angel who redeemed me from all evil, May He bless the boys, and may they be called by my name, and by the name of my fathers, Abraham and Isaac. May they multiply to a multitude in the midst of the land."

Torah Portion Outline

Genesis Chapter 47:28-32
- Carry Me Out of Egypt.

Genesis Chapter 48:1-21
- Jacob Blesses Ephraim and Manasseh.

Genesis Chapter 49:1-33
- Jacob Blesses His Sons Before His Death.

Genesis Chapter 50:1-14
- The People Mourn for Jacob, **Gen.50:1-14**
- Joseph Speaks Kindly to His Brothers, **Gen.50:14-26**

LESSON SUMMARY:

The life of Joseph was a big surprise to all his brothers. Joseph was seventeen years old when his brothers sold him into slavery and lied to their father that he was killed by a wild animal. Little did they know that was a part of God's plan to bring Joseph into Egypt to preserve their lives during the time of famine. Over the past few weeks, we have seen the dreams that Joseph had about his brothers and parents bowing down to him come to pass as they came to Egypt to buy food and also when they came to live in Egypt. We learned in the Torah Portion, Vayigash, Jacob, and all his sons and their children, came to Egypt to live. They lived in the best part of Egypt known as Goshen. This Torah Portion tells us that Jacob lived seventy years in Egypt before His death. Jacob knew that Egypt was not the land God promised him, and made preparations for his body to be carried out of Egypt when he died. Jacob called his son Joseph and had him swear to take his body and bury him in the cave in the field of Machpelah. That was the cave Abraham bought from Ephron the son of Het to bury Sarah. It is also where Abraham and Isaac were buried. It is also the same place where Jacob buried Leah. Joseph swore to Jacob that he will not bury him in Egypt.

Joseph heard that Jacob was sick, so he took his two sons, Ephraim and Manasseh to visit him. When Jacob saw the boys he blessed them and declared that they would be remembered forever.

THE FAMILY BLESSING
Genesis 49: 1-28 The Message Bible

49 Jacob called his sons and said, "Gather around. I want to tell you what you can expect in the days to come." **2** Come together, listen sons of Jacob, listen to Israel your father. **3-4** Reuben, you're my firstborn, my strength, first proof of my manhood, at the top in honor and at the top in power, But like a bucket of water spilled, you'll be at the top no more, Because you climbed into your father's marriage bed, mounting that couch, and you defiled it. **5-6** Simeon and Levi are two of a kind, ready to fight at the drop of a hat. I don't want anything to do with their vendettas, want no part in their bitter feuds; They kill men in fits of temper, slash oxen on a whim. **7**

A curse on their uncontrolled anger, on their indiscriminate wrath. I'll throw them out with the trash; I'll shred and scatter them like confetti throughout Israel. **8-12** You, Judah, your brothers will praise you: Your fingers on your enemies' throat, while your brothers honor you. You're a lion's cub, Judah, home fresh from the kill, my son. Look at him, crouched like a lion, king of beasts; who dares mess with him? The scepter shall not leave Judah; he'll keep a firm grip on the command staff until the ultimate ruler comes and the nations obey him. He'll tie up his donkey to the grapevine, his purebred prize to a sturdy branch. He will wash his shirt in wine and his cloak in the blood of grapes, His eyes will be darker than wine, his teeth whiter than milk. **13** Zebulun settles down on the seashore; he's a safe harbor for ships, right alongside Sidon. **14-15** Issachar is one tough donkey crouching between the corrals; When he saw how good the place was, how pleasant the country, He gave up his freedom and went to work as a slave. **16-17** Dan will handle matters of justice for his people; he will hold his own just fine among the tribes of Israel. Dan is only a small snake in the grass, a lethal serpent in ambush by the road when he strikes a horse in the heel, and brings its huge rider crashing down. **18** I wait in hope for your salvation, God. **19** Gad will be attacked by bandits, but he will trip them up. **20** Asher will become famous for rich foods, candies and sweets fit for kings. **21-26** Naphtali is a deer running free that gives birth to lovely fawns. Joseph is a wild donkey, a wild donkey by a spring, spirited donkeys on a hill. The archers with malice attacked, shooting their hate-tipped arrows; But he held steady under fire, his bow firm, his arms limber, With the backing of the Champion of Jacob, the Shepherd, the Rock of Israel. The God of your father—may he help you! And may The Strong God—may he give you his blessings, Blessings tumbling out of the skies, blessings bursting up from the Earth—blessings of breasts and womb. May the blessings of your father exceed the blessings of the ancient mountains, surpass the delights of the eternal hills; May they rest on the head of Joseph, on the brow of the one consecrated among his brothers. **27** Benjamin is a ravenous wolf; all morning he gorges on his kill, at evening divides up what's left over. **28** All these are the tribes of Israel, the twelve tribes. And this is what their father said to them as he blessed them, blessing each one with his own special farewell blessing.

When Jacob finished speaking to his sons he laid himself in the bed, then he breathed his last breath, and died. All the people of Egypt mourned for Jacob when he died. Joseph's brothers were worried now that their father had died that Joseph would treat them harshly, but Joseph reminded them that he did not hate them for what they did because it was God who used them to fulfill His purpose.

LESSON DISCUSSION:

THE FAMILY BLESSING AND LEGACY

Though Jacob was now living in Egypt he did not forget about the promise God gave him when he had the dream of the ladder with angels ascending and descending on it. Jacob knowing that God would keep His promise, chose to bless his sons, and also the sons of Joseph. Jacob did something very unusual. Jacob did not only bless his grandsons Ephraim and Manasseh, but he also adopted them as his children. Why is this important? Joseph's sons were considered Egyptians because their mother was an Egyptian and they would not have been counted with his other grandchildren to receive an inheritance. Jacob had to make sure that all his descendants were included in the promise of God.

Genesis 48:3-6 3

Then Jacob said to Joseph, "*El Shaddai* appeared to me in Luz, in the land of Canaan, and blessed me." **4** He said to me, 'I am going to make you fruitful and multiply you and turn you into an assembly of peoples, and I will give this land to your seed after you as an everlasting possession.' **5** So now, your two sons, who were born to you in the land of Egypt before I came to you in Egypt, they are mine. Ephraim and Manasseh will be mine, just like Reuben and Simeon. **6** Any descendent of yours whom you father after them will be yours; they will be identified by the names of their brothers for their inheritance.

The legacy continues. Through the blood of Yeshua, we are Adopted into the family of God. It was important for Jacob to bless Ephraim and Manasseh for they to have an inheritance and be included in the multitude of peoples and nations that would come from the promise of God. The promise was not only for Jacob's physical children but also for his spiritual children. Torah tells us that all who believe in Yeshua have been adopted into the family of God. We become heirs of the promise that God gave to Abraham, Isaac, and Jacob.

Ephesians 1:5 NLT (New Living Translation)

God decided in advance to adopt us into his own family by bringing us to Himself through Jesus Christ.

Every son received a special blessing, but the blessing was for the entire family. The purpose of the blessing is so that they will use their strengths to help the family and fulfill God's plan for them to be a great nation. You and I may not receive a special blessing from our natural parents but God has special blessings and gifts for all His children. These gifts and blessings are to be used to help other members of His family, so those who don't know Him will see Him and believe in Him.

Ephesians 4:11-13 NLT

11 Now these are the gifts Christ gave to the church: the apostles, the prophets, the evangelists, and the pastors and teachers. **12** Their responsibility is to equip God's people to do his work and build up the church, the body of Christ. **13** This will continue until we all come to such unity in our faith and knowledge of God's Son that we will be mature in the Lord, measuring up to the full and complete standard of Christ.

TURNING POINT:

GOD USED IT FOR MY GOOD!

Genesis 50: The Message Bible

14-15 After burying his father, Joseph went back to Egypt. All his brothers who had come with him to bury his father returned with him. After the funeral, Joseph's brothers talked among themselves: "What if Joseph is carrying a grudge and decides to pay us back for all the wrong we did him?" **16-17** So they sent Joseph a message, "Before his death, your father gave this command: Tell Joseph, 'Forgive your brothers' sin—all that wrongdoing. They did treat you very badly.' Will you do it? Will you forgive the sins of the servants of your father's God?" When Joseph received their message, he wept. **18** Then the brothers went in person to him, threw themselves on the ground before him and said, "We'll be your slaves." **19-21** Joseph replied, "Don't be afraid. Do I act for God? Don't you see, you planned evil against me but God used those same plans for my good, as you see all around you right now—life for many people. Easy now, you have nothing to fear; I'll take care of you and your children." He reassured them, speaking with them heart-to-heart.

NO NEED FOR REVENGE

There are times in our lives when we are hurt by the actions and words of others; because of the pain we feel we are tempted to do and say something that will make the person also feel pain. As good as it sounds revenge, will not make you feel better. Pain is a natural response to hurt, but we must learn how to deal with pain the Godly way.

If the pain is physical you can get medicine to help heal the pain. When your feelings or emotions are hurt, the best medicine is forgiveness. After their father's death, Joseph could have taken revenge for what his brothers did to him. Instead, Joseph demonstrated forgiveness when his brothers came to him out of fear of what he might do to them because they sold him as a slave.

Joseph was much older and had gained wisdom and understanding from God. He had learned the true meaning of God's love and His purpose in life. Joseph was able to love his brothers because he knew that for everything they did, God used it for his good.

God will always take care of those who love, trust in Him, and keep His commandments. All things (good or bad) will work together for the good of those who love God and are called for His purpose (Romans 8:28).

When someone hurts you, you don't have to worry about taking revenge because God is in control. Learning to forgive someone who hurt you is not always easy, but with the help of the Ruach of HaKodesh (Holy Spirit), it is possible. If you are hurting, now is a good time to ask Him to help you forgive and learn to love the person who caused you pain.

God will one day use your pain to help someone. You will be able to share with someone that God healed your pain and He can heal their pain if they ask Him. Next time you are tempted to take revenge, remember all things work together for the good of those who love God!

PRACTICAL APPLICATIONS
A SPECIAL GIFT FROM GOD

FOR CHILDREN 4-6 YEARS OLD

Ask your parents to pray for you and to write a blessing for you. Keep the blessing as a reminder that you are a gift from God.

FOR CHILDREN 7-12 YEARS OLD

Galatians 5:22-23 – But the Holy Spirit produces this kind of fruit in our lives: love, joy, peace, patience, kindness, goodness, faithfulness, **23** gentleness, and self-control. There is no law against these things!

Ask the Holy Spirit to help you to be an example to your friends and family and share His fruits with them through you.

FOLLOW-UP FROM THE LAST TORAH PORTION

Ask who wants to share from last week's practical application
DEMONSTRATING THE SPIRIT OF TRUTH

FOR CHILDREN 4-6 YEARS OLD

Always tell your parents the truth even when you are afraid of getting in trouble.

FOR CHILDREN 7-12 YEARS OLD

Telling your friends the truth sometimes can hurt their feelings. Ask the Holy Spirit to teach you how to speak the truth in love and with kindness.

QUESTIONS - TEACHERS ANSWER KEY

1. **How old was Joseph when he was sold into Egypt?**
   17 years old

2. **How many years did Jacob live in Egypt before his death?**
   17 years

3. **Who was adopted by Jacob?**
   Ephraim and Manasseh

4. **Who is Jacob's firstborn son?**
   Reuben

5. **Which two brothers did Jacob say are two of a kind?**
   Simeon and Levi

6. **Which son is like a ravenous wolf?**
   Benjamin

7. **Who was called a wild donkey?**
   Joseph

8. **Who would settle by the seashore?**
   Zebulun

9. **From which son did Jacob say the ultimate rule (Yeshua) would come?**
   Judah

10. **Which son is small and is compared to a snake in the grass?**
    Dan

QUESTIONS - CHILDREN'S COPY

1. How old was Joseph when he was sold into Egypt?

2. How many years did Jacob live in Egypt before his death?

3. Who was adopted by Jacob?

4. Who is Jacob's firstborn son?

5. Which two brothers did Jacob say are two of a kind?

6. Which son is like a ravenous wolf?

7. Who was called a wild donkey?

8. Who would settle by the seashore?

9. From which son did Jacob say the ultimate rule (Yeshua) would come?

10. Which son is small and is compared to a snake in the grass?

CRAFTS FOR TORAH PORTION VAYECHI

SUPPLIES:

1. 12x12 Cardstock paper of various colors.
2. Plain paper for drawing/printing
3. Markers/crayons/pencils
4. Glue stick
5. Gems

CRAFTS: 12 Tribes of Israel
The children will learn about 12 sons/tribes and the symbols corresponding to them.

1. First, each child will receive individual drawings of all 12 sons. They will glue them on 2 12x12 card stock papers (colors vary), 6 on each card stock.

2. Then the children will need to guess which symbol belongs to which tribe. A teacher will show the drawing and the children will guess next to which of the 12 brothers to glue it on.

3. After they are done with all 12, they will color the drawings.

4. Finish with decorating the tribe of Levi's breastplate with gems.

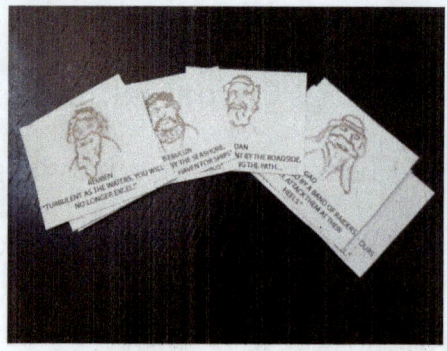

About the Authors

Natalee Henry began her personal faith journey in 1996 with a burning desire to live an extraordinary life for the Lord. Since then, the Lord has kindled a passion within her for sharing and teaching the Word of God.

In 2016, God answered Natalee's prayer for spiritual growth when she was introduced to studying, learning, and implementing the Torah way of life as a believer in Yeshua. Natalee is a Torah-observant believer learning to honor God's Appointed Times and serving within her local congregation to all ages.

Natalee is an author, motivational speaker, and founder of the Season Destiny Ministry designed to *"**empower youths to make the right decisions in life.**"* Natalee is a graduate of International Seminary Bible College, and authored **Seasons of Life-Taking Man Back To God**, 2005; **Embracing Destiny**, 2010; **Overcome to Fulfill Your Purpose: Become Successfully You**, and **Successfully You, Leadership Training Workbook** 2018, and her most recent, **Making Transition Through Crisis: A Rebuilding Guide for Young Professionals**, 2021.

Natalee has a passion for young people and seeks to share with them that they do not have to 'settle' for being less than God created them to be; nor do they need to succumb to today's culture, lies, and worldliness.

 **Yevgeniya Calendrillo** was born and raised in Ukraine to a secular Jewish family. Growing up, Yevgeniya yearned for a relationship with God for many years. By the age of 24, she was married and living in the United States. Yevgeniya and her husband are entrepreneurs and business partners selling their artwork and also are heavily focused on nutrition and health. Yevgeniya and her husband have one son, whom she homeschooled for 3 1/2 years.

Yevgeniya was invited to a Messianic congregation in Brooklyn where she accepted Yeshua as her Savior; and opened the Bible for the very first time. Yevgeniya has been a Messianic believer for over 20 years.

Yevgniya has a Bachelor's degree in Fashion Design from the Fashion Institute of Technology, New York. Yevgeniya has many years of experience in the New York fashion industry. Yevgniya is an artist who is gifted in watercolor painting. She recently discovered her talent for children's crafts and utilizes her knowledge, and experience in arts and design, as tools for investing in children for the Kingdom of God. Yevgeniya is currently serving as Children's Ministry Leader and a children's Torah teacher at Save The Nations.

Yevgeniya has a passion to follow God, to be obedient to His Torah instructions, to seek Him diligently, and to walk in her calling to teach Torah and Hebrew lessons to children.

About the Book

B'reisheet (Book 1: Genesis) is a part of the Torah Curriculum for children, covering the first five books of the Bible. This curriculum is based on the weekly Torah Portions so they may learn Torah in a simple and practical way.

The Lessons are structured so our children will learn from the Torah Portions and see the connection with Yeshua (Jesus), and the work of the Holy Spirit. Our aim is not just to give information but to teach Torah principles and demonstrate how to use them in their lives.

Each lesson is designed as a guide for teaching the Torah Portions to children ages 4 to 12 years. This curriculum is filled with creative crafts designed by Yevgeniya and insightful lessons written by Natalee.

Coming Soon

Shemot - Book 2: Exodus
Vayikra - Book 3: Leviticus
Bamidbar - Book 4: Numbers
Devarim - Book 5: Deuteronomy

Visit our website at www.torah4children.net to learn more about other books from our curriculum and our ministry.

www.ingramcontent.com/pod-product-compliance
Lightning Source LLC
Chambersburg PA
CBHW060300240426
43661CB00060B/2849